opposing viewpoints

foreign policy

1985 supplement

David L. Bender, *Publisher*
Bruno Leone, *Executive Editor*
M. Teresa O'Neill, *Senior Editor*
Claudia Bialke Debner, *Editor*
Bonnie Szumski, *Editor*
Lynn Hall, *Assistant Editor*
Susan Bursell, *Assistant Editor*
Janelle Rohr, *Assistant Editor*

David Owen Kieft, Ph.D., *Consulting Editor*
Associate Professor of History
University of Minnesota, Minneapolis

greenhaven press, inc.

577 Shoreview Park Road
St. Paul, MN 55126

© 1985 by Greenhaven Press, Inc.

ISBN 0-89908-510-5

ISSN 0748-2841

contents

Editors' Note

Opposing Viewpoints SOURCES provide a wealth of opinions on important issues of the day. The annual supplements focus on the topics that continue to generate debate. Readers will find that *Opposing Viewpoints SOURCES* become exciting barometers of today's controversies. This is achieved in three ways. First, by expanding previous chapters with the most current opinions on the chapter topics. Second, by adding new materials which are timeless in nature. And third, by adding recent topical issues not dealt with in previous volumes or supplements.

Viewpoints

Terrorism

101. **Capitalist Countries Sponsor Terrorism**   1
by David A. Michaels, Yuri Gvozdev, & Daily World

The US has a history of terrorism unmatched by most of the world, which makes it a prolific exporter of terrorist tactics. The Soviet Union is against terrorism and believes in universally accepted principles and standards of conduct.

102. **Totalitarian Countries Sponsor Terrorism** *by Jeane J. Kirkpatrick*   5

Terrorists and totalitarians have ideology in common. Both attempt to confuse as well as to terrorize, so it is natural for totalitarian countries to contribute toward terrorism.

103. **Anti-Terrorist Actions Will Protect US Citizens** *by Samuel T. Francis*   9

Government-sponsored covert action against extremist groups would be highly effective in disrupting and reducing terrorist activities against US citizens.

104. **Anti-Terrorist Actions Threaten US Human Rights** *by* The People   11

The government tactics planned for anti-terrorist activities are contrary to basic American political values and traditions.

105. **Terrorism Is Controllable** *by Noel C. Koch*   13

Government actions against terrorism will continue to prevent most successful attacks until terrorist groups ultimately lose their fervor.

106. **Terrorism Is Uncontrollable** *by Glenn Garvin*   17

The immense rise in international terrorism in the 80s indicates that no effective means have been developed to curtail or control it.

107. **The US Should Seek Rapprochment with Terrorist States** *by Robin Wright*   21

The use of force against the states with government-sponsored terrorism is risky and dangerous. A far more viable approach is to acknowledge their ideologies and their right to exist.

108. **The US Should Leave Terrorist States** *by Charles William Maynes*   25

The best approach to state-sponsored terrorism in the Middle East is to send the US military and civilians home until the situation improves. The US presence is only exacerbating the tension.

109. **The US Should Punish Terrorist States** *by Paul Johnson*   29

Terrorism is a malignancy that feeds on the hesitations and visions endemic to liberal societies. The US should have the courage to strike at the heart of terrorism.

US/Africa

110. **The Ethiopian Famine: An Overview** *by Russ Watson, et al.*   33

The famine in Ethiopia is one of the worst in history. Millions are in need of food, medical help and, in the long run, agricultural education and supplies.

111. **Communism Caused the Ethiopian Famine** *by Robert W. Lee*   37

The famine in Ethiopia is man-made. The inept communist government squandered resources and allowed the starvation to reach a crisis point.

112. **Population Growth Caused the Ethiopian Famine** by *Lester Brown* 41
The Ethiopian drought is not the primary cause of the Ethiopian famine. An unchecked population effects the climate and land use, making land less productive.

113. **Apartheid Remains an Inhumane System** by *Desmond Tutu* 45
The apartheid system creates poverty and despair for blacks. The US should use its influence to try to overturn the system.

114. **Disinvestment Would Aid South African Blacks** by *James North* 49
Far from being inhumane and relentless, apartheid is changing. There is much less racial segregation than ever before.

115. **Apartheid Is Improving** by *Otto Ulc* 55
South African blacks would be helped by US disinvestment. Quiet diplomacy has not worked, and the US needs to take more of a stand against apartheid.

116. **Disinvestment Would Hurt South African Blacks** by *The Lincoln Review* 59
Apartheid is changing for the better. American disinvestment would lead to massive black unemployment which would force South African blacks to revolt. This would cause a much worse situation for blacks than exists under apartheid.

117. **US Corporations Can Change Apartheid** 63
by *Leon H. Sullivan & William J. Choyke*
Corporations have affected minor changes in apartheid already. They can continue to become even more of a force for change in the future.

118. **US Corporations Cannot Change South Africa** by *Clifton R. Wharton* 67
The US has long maintained that its corporations improve the conditions in South Africa. This is only a myth. Conditions continue to worsen, and the US has no excuse for remaining.

US/Central America

119. **The US Should Not Aid the Contras** by *McGeorge Bundy* 69
Using contras to overthrow the Nicaraguan government will not work and will discredit the US government. US-backed contra warfare damages national interest by making the Sandinista government more authoritarian and militaristic.

120. **The US Should Aid the Contras** by *Mark Falcoff* 71
Supporting the contras will pressure the Nicaraguan government to be more democratic. If the United states conducts foreign policy without the option of threatening military action, its role will be limited to giving money to Third World countries in hopes of favorably influencing them while communists, including the Sandinistas, use US money to make revolutions.

121. **The Reagan Doctrine: An Overview** by *Doyle McManus* 75
Debate about the Reagan Doctrine centers around the issues of what type of support the United States should offer rebels fighting communism, whether the aid should be overt or covert, and what standards the United States should use for determining whether a rebel movement deserves support.

122. **The Reagan Doctrine Is Sound** by *Charles Krauthammer* 79
Supporting popular revolts against tyrannous governments had been an American tradition until the Vietnam war. The Reagan Doctrine restores that tradition and recognizes that sovereignty is neither a moral issue nor absolute.

123. **The Reagan Doctrine Is Wrong** by *Eric Patterson* & In These Times 83
The United States should respect third world countries sovereignty, even when those countries make decisions contrary to US interests. The Reagan Doctrine will only push the Sandinistas further into the Soviet orbit.

124. **The US Is the Victim of a Propoganda Campaign** by *the US State Department* 87
The Nicaraguan propanda campaign has created misperceptions about the US role in Central America. The United States supports democracy and has tried to negotiate with the Sandinista government. The Sandinistas have not kept their promises of pluralism, a mixed economy, and non-alignment.

125. **Nicaragua Is the Victim of a Propaganda Campaign** by *Phillip Berryman* 93
To justify military intervention, the Reagan administration has been conducting a campaign of distortions and half-truths against the Nicaraguan government. The Sandinistas are not Marxist totalitarians aligned with the Soviets. Most Nicaraguans support the Sandinista government.

Bibliography B-1

Index I-1

"The dropping of atomic bombs on two cities in Japan constituted acts of terrorism."

viewpoint 101

Capitalist Countries Sponsor Terrorism

David A. Michaels, Yuri Gvozdev, & *Daily World*

Editor's note: The following viewpoint is taken from three newspaper editorials in the Daily World. *Part I is by David A. Michaels, part II is by Yuri Gvozdev, and part III is written by a* Daily World *staff writer.*

I

Terrorism is commonly understood to be the indiscriminate killing or injury of human beings. It is condemned as being heartless, harming the innocent as well as the guilty. Nevertheless, terrorism is not always an individual act. It can be sanctioned by a government, officially or unofficially, as part of its policy. The murders and rapes in Nicaragua, perpetrated by the contras, furnish a case in point.

The capitalist elite, through their control of the media, try to convince the public that "radicals" are behind terrorist acts. Newspapers, films, radio, television, and magazines—all attempt to picture terrorism as the actions of left-wing assassins. Actually, the precise opposite is the truth. What we are shown is the mirror image of what the capitalists do. No one can be as cruel and vicious as a right-winger. Death squads and torture chambers are commonplace in the world of free enterprise, whether in El Salvador or in Chile. Of course, in fascist Spain and in Hitler's Germany, they were officially sponsored by the government.

Centuries ago, the armed knights known as Crusaders were blessed by religious leaders as they rode forth to smite down the "infidel Saracens."In Spain, holy men were in charge of the torture chambers called the Inquisition. Throughout Europe, in the Middle Ages, the small aristocratic class exploited and abused the bulk of the population. Any dissidents who complained were beaten or killed. The rape of peasant women by their lords was considered normal.

What about the U.S.? What is our record?

The original settlers on our continent were, of course, the Indians. Onto their soil came the intruders, the English, the French, the Spanish, and other adventurers looking for gold and wealth. Peaceful Indians were overcome by the muskets and the horses of the European explorers, and resistance was smashed with mass killings. Were these not terrorist acts? Even later in our country's history, the white men constantly broke treaties that they had made with the Indians and persecuted them.

Perhaps the greatest act of terrorism in our country came in the establishment of a system of slavery. Black men and women became mere chattel, objects to be bought and sold. A man would be taken from his wife and family and shipped somewhere as if he were a piece of furniture. Slaves could be whipped and beaten and killed. The racism which still persists in the U.S. is a legacy of that dreadful period when human rights were denied to the slaves. Even today, we have a secret and insidious form of terrorism against the poor, denying them the decencies of life and holding them up to public scorn.

Lenin and the other pioneers of Socialism constantly warned against individual acts of terrorism. An oppressed people, they stated, may fight for its freedom. Terrorist acts, on the other hand, will only jeopardize the mass actions of the people for their liberty. What is needed is the mobilization of workers and peasants in an organized way. Individual terrorism may serve merely to distract from the struggle, and may alienate possible supporters.

Re-Education Camps

When Vietnam achieved its independence, after many years of battling against the French and the U.S., our media warned us against an impending "bloodbath." Of course, no such thing happened. The former members of the police and the military, who

David A. Michaels, "The Real Face of Terrorism," *Daily World*, November 30, 1984. *Daily World*, "Welcoming Terrorists," December 12, 1984. Yuri Gvozdev, "State-sponsored Terrorism," *Daily World*, October 12, 1984.

had oppressed the population, were sent instead to re-education camps. Socialists believe in the human ability to learn and to change. Only the most warped and intractable members of the oppressing group, who had been hired by the elite, remain in detention.

We may contrast this situation with events in Chile. After the CIA, working with U.S. industrialists, had managed to overthrow the elected Allende government, the right wingers ruthlessly hunted down all opposition: students, intellectuals, unionists, and others who might resist the Pinochet dictatorship. Thousands of people were murdered, without protest from the U.S. government. Here was a real case of terrorism.

"[US]-sponsored terrorism and armed provocations by foreign forces continue against Vietnam, Laos and Kampuchea."

The dropping of atomic bombs on two cities in Japan constituted acts of terrorism. The bomb that fell on Hiroshima could just as well have been exploded in an unoccupied area to demonstrate its awesome qualities. When British and U.S. planes utterly destroyed the city of Dresden in a fire-bombing attack (killing more people than in Japan), was this not an act of terrorism? After all, Dresden had no military significance, and was mainly a civilian area. When U.S. battleships fired their huge guns, allegedly to wipe out the PLO headquarters in Lebanon, did they not know full well that the shells would kill many civilians? Was this not an act of terrorism?

CIA Incident

Perhaps the most ghastly incident involving terrorism occured in Indonesia. In the 1960's, under Eisenhower, the CIA tried to overthrow the regime of Sukarno.

President Sukarno tried to arm people against a possible right-wing coup. Aided by the CIA, the rightists struck. The carnage was indescribable. Rivers ran red with the bodies floating in the water. Again, students, unionists, intellectuals, and peasant leaders were slaughtered. Estimates ranged from a half million to a million who were killed.

Of course, these terrorists were "good" ones, so that our U.S. government did not demonstrate its horror over the slaughter. In fact, we were quick to recognize the new government of Suharto. Evidently, the murders in Indonesia were in the highest traditions of monopoly capitalism.

The lesson is that we must reject the idea that terrorism is a product of radical thought. We must point out to our friends and neighbors what the real face of terrorism looks like. And we must organize to eliminate such depravity.

II

At the UN, the Soviet Union has introduced an initiative which may play a major role in improving the world situation. It has proposed for inclusion in the agenda of the current 39th session of the UN General Assembly an item on the inadmissibility of policies of state-sponsored terrorism and any actions by states aimed at undermining the socio-political systems in other sovereign states. The Soviet Union streses the importance of urgency of considering this proposal.

The letter by Andrei Gromyko to Javier Perez de Cuellar, UN secretary-general, notes that certain states, in trying to achieve military superiority and pursuing a policy of terrorism in international affairs, have been resorting ever more frequently to actions designed to undermine the socio-political systems of other states and going so far as to use arms.

The U.S. particularly adheres to such a method in its relations with other countries. In the most open form this has been displayed in the gangster-like attack on the Pentagon's troops in October 1983 on the tiny island state of Grenada with the further occupation of that country. Why has this been done? The Reagan administration did not like the non-alignment policy of the Maurice Bishop government, its course towards deep-going social changes.

CIA Mercenaries

Another example is the undeclared war waged by the CIA mercenaries against Nicaragua—the real military, economic and political siege of that country staged by Washington. What is the reason for this? Managua's independent foreign policy and the restructuring of society on the basis of genuine democracy and social justice are not to U.S. liking.

Out of the same selfish, imperial considerations the Reagan administration helps its proteges in El Salvador to carry out genocide, to wage a war against their own people. This policy of state-sponsored terrorism has its rich pre-history in the region.

Many observers in the U.S. itself note the striking invariability of the U.S. policy in Central America and in the Caribbean area over the past 90 years. In other words, the main components of present state-sponsored terrorism were already tested at the turn of the 19th and 20th centuries when either the USSR or socialist Cuba did not exist, although the U.S. is trying to justify its own arbitrariness south of its borders by references to the "threat" posed by these countries to the Western hemisphere.

The US and Non-Interference

It can be concluded that the U.S. comes out in the region against all who uphold the sovereign right of their countries for self-determination and non-interference.

Of late, the Reagan administration has been aggressively trying to spread such experience to the whole globe. It spends hundreds of millions of dollars on the undeclared war against Afghanistan in order to throw the people of that country back to the Middle Ages, is trying to compel Lebanon to surrender to Israel and to establish an order in that country which would be suitable to Washington. State-sponsored terrorism and armed provocations by foreign forces continue against Vietnam, Laos and Kampuchea.

Such policy and actions, which are a violation of the elementary international norms of conduct and ethics, are especially dangerous in the nuclear age. Under modern conditions they can have harmful consequences not only for the freedom of peoples, but also for their very existence. It is particularly dangerous when the U.S., for instance, artificially tries to impart a global character to its imperial adventure in Central America or Asia and to interpret its aggressive violence over a sovereign country as "East-West confrontation," as "struggle against Communist expansion," etc.

Observing the UN Charter

The Soviet Union believes that the interests of preserving peace require that ideological differences should not be brought into inter-state relations and that they should be based on the strict observance of the UN charter and the universally accepted principles and standards of conduct in the world arena.

The Soviet initiative, which calls on the UN to resolutely denounce the policy and practice of state-sponsored terrorism, is widely welcomed in the world. The time has come for the UN to call on all states to fully respect the right of peoples to choose their socio-political systems freely, without foreign interference, to carry out their socio-economic development in compliance with their own aims and needs. This would greatly contribute to the creation of the political guarantees of peace, to the strengthening of the security of individual states and to the consolidation of international security.

III

The State Department has announced that it will give Roberto d'Aubuisson, a key figure behind El Salvador's right-wing death squads, a visa to enter the U.S. and meet with prominent rightists in Washington. It does this despite the fact that death squads in El Salvador, in addition to killing countless numbers of Salvadorans, have also murdered several U.S. citizens.

The decision to extend these visas to the terrorist leader comes only a short time after the State Department denied visas to four Salvadoran women who were to travel to Washington to receive the Robert F. Kennedy Prize for work in the area of human rights.

This is the second time d'Aubuisson has been granted a visa by the State Department. Apparently the administration would prefer to welcome those who aid in the murder of U.S. citizens than those who would work to end the slaughter.

The Domestic Ultra-Right

Key to the decision to put out the welcome mat for d'Aubuisson is the role of the right-wing terrorist's allies in the U.S.—the domestic ultra-right. Thus, d'Aubuisson is to be honored at a dinner given by conservative groups that supported the president's re-election.

Even more important than narrow political considerations, however, is U.S. strategy in the region. At a time when the puppet government in El Salvador is hardening its position in negotiations with liberation fighters, the Reagan administration is bolstering the number one opponent of peaceful talks in that country. Apparently the right wing in the U.S. continues to bank on a military solution—despite the fact that such a course could well throw the entire region into a deadly struggle that could expand into a world-wide confrontation. This visa is another sign that intensification of the peace struggle is critical.

Definition of Terror

According to Webster's New World Dictionary, the word "terror" means "the use of violence to intimidate . . . used especially as a political weapon or policy." Supposedly, the FBI spends millions of dollars a year countering terrorism. . . .

"What is 'terrorist,' according to the FBI, are the activities of civil rights and peace activists and fighters for social progress."

What is "terrorist," according to the FBI, are the activities of civil rights and peace activists and fighters for social progress. During the 1950s and 1960s, thousands of progressives were illegally jailed or harassed by the FBI. Today, activists continue to be investigated and harassed by the agency regularly.

Only a public outcry over truly terrorist incidents like clinic bombings, racial and anti-Semitic violence, and other violent acts against the working people, will assure justice.

David A. Michaels authored an article on terrorism for the Daily World, *a communist labor newspaper. Yuri Gvozdev is a political anaylst for the Novosti Press Agency.*

"Both terrorists and totalitarians act and see themselves as acting in the name of a new morality and on the basis of a different epistemology."

viewpoint**102**

Totalitarian Countries Sponsor Terrorism

Jeane J. Kirkpatrick

The most difficult problem in understanding politics is, I believe, to see the phenomena as they are without confusion or mystification, simply to observe who does what to whom, to hear what he says about his actions, and to observe their consequences. The more simply and clearly the phenomena can be observed and described, the greater the possibility that their meaning and significance can be understood.

What the terrorist does is kill, maim, kidnap, torture. His victims may be children in the schoolroom, travelers like those held and rescued at Entebbe, or gathered in an airport as at Lod. They may be industrialists returning home from work, political leaders—diplomats in Paris, London, Los Angeles—or legislators like those on whom machine guns were turned in the 1950s here in Washington. The terrorist's victims may have no particular political identity—like the cafe-goers at Goldenberger's in Paris or the passers-through at Lod (now Ben Gurion Airport); or they may be political symbols, like Aldo Moro or, perhaps, Pope John Paul II. They may be kidnapped and held for ransom, maimed or simply blown to bits. One defining characteristic of the terrorist is his choice of method: the terrorist chooses violence as the instrument of first resort.

Yet terrorism is distinguished from violent crime. Crime, too, is unauthorized violence against persons who are not at war. How does terrorism differ from simple crime? The difference lies not in the nature of the act, but in the understanding of the perpetrator, however vague, about what he is doing. Terrorism is *political* in a way that crime is not; the terrorist acts in the name of some political, some public purpose. Political man, Harold Lasswell wrote, is one who

Jeane J. Kirkpatrick, from an address at the Jonathan Institute's Conference on International Terrorism held in Washington, DC, June 25, 1984.

projects *private* affects onto public objects and rationalizes them in the name of a conception of the public good. The members of Murder, Inc. acted for private purposes. John Hinckley, as I understand it, attempted to kill President Reagan for essentially private reasons. But the killers who sprayed bullets into Goldenberger's, like those who attempted to murder Eden Pastora, had a public goal in view. Terrorism is a form of political war. While the conception of the actor transforms the act, and while a purpose related to a public goal makes an act political, it does not make it moral. A public purpose does not make a terrorist who has been arrested a political prisoner.

Soldier Violence

Terrorism should also be distinguished from conventional war and terrorists from soldiers who wield violence. A soldier wields violence in accordance with the legal authorities of his society against enemies designated by legally constituted authorities. Soldiers use violence where a state of belligerence is recognized to exist. The terrorist engages in violence in violation of law against persons who are not at war with him. Even in this century of total war, when civilian targets are drawn into conflict by bombing and by resistance movements, belligerency is at least a condition known to all the parties to a conflict. The Nazi occupiers patrolling the streets of Paris understood that French civilians were not only conquered but, that for many, the war continued. They understood that some unknown portion of the civilian population was at war with them and had not acquiesced in the surrender signed by France's wartime government.

Terrorists use violence against people who do not understand themselves to be at war. The victims of terrorist attack are unarmed, undefended and unwary. They may be, in my opinion, sleeping Marines on a peace-keeping mission, or an industrialist coming home from work or schoolchildren in their schoolroom. The point is, and it seems to me crucial, the victims conceive themselves as civilians. They do not understand that they are regarded, or may be regarded, by someone else as belligerents in an ongoing war. This is a reason that one study done in our government emphasized that terrorism is "politically motivated, premeditated violence perpetrated against non-combatant targets by subnational groups or clandestine state agents."

"Terrorists and totalitarians alike thrive on falsification and intimidation."

If we listen to the terrorist, we understand that he is at war against us. Terrorism is a form of war against a society and all who embody it. War, as always, is as Clausewitz emphasized, "a real political instrument, a continuation of politics by other means." It is an "an act of violence intended to compel our opponent to fulfill our will."

Absolute War
Terrorist war is part of a total war which sees the whole of society as the enemy, and *all* the members of a society as appropriate objects for violent action. It is absolute war, because its goal is absolute destruction of a society and because it accepts annihilation of persons as an appropriate means. Terrorists are the shock troops in a war to the death against the values and institutions of a society— Western society or non-Western society—and of the people who embody it.

The terrorist does not necessarily possess a comprehensive doctrine or plan. It is only necessary that he relate his violent act to a social political goal. In our times he is likely also to be linked to an organization of others who share his understood "political" interests and who organize and assist his violent acts and relate them to international political goals.

The affinities between terrorism and totalitarianism are multiple. Both politicize the whole of society—the totalitarian by making society, culture and personality the object of his plans, actions and power, the terrorist by taking the whole of society as the object and enemy of his violence, his war. Both conceive violence as an appropriate means to their political ends and use violence as an instrument of first resort aggressively. They understand that smashing a society means smashing people. Both reject basic moral principles associated with Judeo-Christian civilization, such as the value and responsibility of the individual, and also reject prohibitions against the use of offensive force in social or international affairs. "We are against everything that is good and decent," said home-grown terrorist Bernadine Dorhn.

Both terrorists and totalitarians act and see themselves as acting in the name of a new morality and on the basis of a different epistemology. Both see their violence as justified by their "higher" morality whose transcendent collective ends justify and demand violation of conventional morality and the sacrifice of people whose membership in the old society makes them "expendable." Both permit and even encourage expression of aggressive, murderous instincts whose repression, Freud correctly emphasized, is a precondition of civilization. The social relations of both to outsiders is dominated by hostile intent. The enemy is everywhere, struggle is inevitable. It is unending. It is total.

Totalitarian Terrorism
But despite the many affinities of terrorism and totalitarianism, the two need also to be distinguished. Totalitarianism is the property of a certain kind of society or polity. One of the instruments of the polity is terror. Terrorism, on the other hand, may be the property of individuals, small groups or governments which do not in fact possess total power, whose rulers may have totalitarian aspirations, but whose societies have not yet become totalitarian. I take it that both Libya and Syria are examples of such states.

Raymond Aron described three kinds of terror as present in the Soviet experience: that used by a party or faction against parties or factions hostile to them; that which aims at eliminating class enemies, such as liquidation of the Kulaks as a class; and that which turned terror previously used against class enemies or adversaries against all those who disagreed with the ruler. This third category permitted anyone who was in any way objectionable to be classified as an "enemy of the people." All these categories of terror are present in the violence of the terrorist. Totalitarian society is saturated with coercion. Nonetheless, not all coercive societies are totalitarian and not all societies that support, sponsor or harbor terrorists and terrorism are totalitarian.

Rejection of Democracy
The most important relations between terrorism and totalitarianism seem to me to be, first, that the most important totalitarian state of our times is also the principal supporter and sponsor of international terrorism as a form of political action; and second, that those who pursue power by terrorism aspire to found totalitarian societies. Orwell wrote: "It is not merely that 'power corrupts,' so also do the ways of attaining power. Therefore all efforts to regenerate society by *violent means* lead to the cellars of the O.G.P.U." "The essential act," he wrote also, "is the rejection of democracy—that is, of the underlying values of democracy; once you have decided that,

Stalin—or at any rate someone *like* Stalin—is already underway."

In Nicaragua, rejection of democracy by the Sandinista junta and the choice of the method of violence has led indeed to something like Stalinism—a system that has forced Miskito Indians into internment camps or exile, has imposed prior censorship, absorbed free trade unions, controlled businessmen, repressed the church and church leaders, and sees Nicaraguans who want a voice in their own governments as "enemies of the people."

It happened, too, in Grenada, where Maurice Bishop and his colleagues seized power by force and attempted to create on that tropical island a full-blown totalitarian state. It happened, of course, in Vietnam where the North imposed a "military solution" on the South and followed its victory with the establishment of totalitarian institutions which have forced hundreds of thousands of South Vietnamese into labor camps for "re-education," driven others into the sea and pressed thousands of others into armies conducting their ongoing permanent war against Cambodia. Something like Stalinism has led to the liquidation of a nation.

The "Armed Road"

The choice of method is the essential political act. It is hardly surprising that rulers who choose coercion as an instrument of government should see violence as a central instrument of government. Beginning in the late 1960s, for example, the Soviet Union and Soviet terrorists began to identify the "armed road," as they called it, as the way to power in the Western hemisphere. They not only discovered that their own experiences could be applied elsewhere; they set about applying those experiences in this hemisphere—the Bandera Roja, FARC, M-19, Sendero Luminoso, FSLN, FMLN, ERP, the Monteneros, the Tupamaros, the MIR, to name just a few of the small bands of violent men, technicians in violence and propaganda, who found ready, external support in their effort to win power by violence over unwilling societies.

They begin with terror and seek, as the definition proposed at the last conference sponsored by the Jonathan Institute has suggested, to inspire fear through the use of terror to gain political ends. Such deliberate use of terror is relied upon to produce a revolutionary situation. It has become the preferred tactic in contemporary revolutionary conflicts. This now familiar cycle is accompanied by a chorus of moral outrage from a self-designated constituency of Soviet client states. They seek to win symbolic support for the violence used in the pursuit of total and absolute power. These "technicians in violence" and propaganda, head what are called "national liberation movements." The Soviets frankly acknowledge that their support for these movements may be decisive as, for example, when they say:

National liberation struggle is a form of war waged by peoples of colonial and dependent or formerly colonial territories in which Socialist countries become the decisive factor when peoples launch an armed struggle against internal reactionaries.

"National liberation movements" is the name given to groups supported by the Soviet Union and associated states seeking power by violence. Their acceptance as legitimate by and in the United States is as good an indicator as any of the moral confusion which has come to surround the use of violence and the choice of violence as the method of political action.

Terrorism for Liberation

Inside the United Nations, beginning in the 1970s, successive majorities of the General Assembly have passed resolutions asserting their support for the right of SWAPO, the PLO, and other national liberation movements "in their struggle, by all means, including armed struggle..." to achieve power. Inside the United Nations, the majorities, forged in blocs, many of whose over-lapping members are Soviet-client states, proclaim the right of these national liberation movements to use all means including violence. The same majorities deny that their intended victims and targets have the right to defend themselves. Thus, Abu Eain, accused of planting a bomb in a teeming market area in Tiberias, Israel—a bomb that killed two boys and injured some thirty others—was treated by the General Assembly as a mere political dissident whose right to dissent and asylum should have been protected by the American courts, whose protections, I may say, he made full use of for a period of years.

"'National liberation movements' is the name given to groups supported by the Soviet Union and associated states seeking power by violence."

The General Assembly denounced the various U.S. court decisions, including that of the U.S. Supreme Court, that held that Abu Eain should be extradicted for trial in Israel. When American courts concluded that bombing of civilians was not a political, and hence non-extractable offense, but rather constituted the crimes of murder and attempted murder and that the perpetrator was subject to prosecution and punishment in the state where the crimes were committed, the United Nations General Assembly reaffirmed, in effect, that terrorism in defense of national liberation is no crime and that the intended victims have no rights of self-defense.

In the semantics of UN majorities today, the distinction between legitimate and illegitimate use of force has not so much been blurred as stood on its head. Where traditionally states are seen as having a monopoly on the legitimate use of violence, UN majorities today see liberation movements as having a monopoly on legitimate use of force against targeted states. According to this upside-down view of terrorism, the peoples whose homes and villages are burned, whose school-children are bombed, whose crops are destroyed, whose cattle are killed, whose leaders are murdered and whose families are forcibly relocated may not be seen as victims of illegitimate violence, but rather as objects of national liberation. Only governments that seek to repress the violence of national liberation movements are cited for human rights violations. In this view, a targeted society has no rights of self-defense against armed bands within its midst.

"Only governments that seek to repress the violence of national liberation movements are cited for human rights violations."

But it cannot be that the Federal Republic of Germany has no right to defend itself against the Baader-Meinhof gang; that the Italian government has no right to defend itself against the Red Brigades; that the government of Spain has no right to defend itself against Basque terrorists; that the government of El Salvador has no right of self-defense against guerrillas who boycott its elections, attack its co-ops, murder its peasants; or that the government of Uruguay has no right to defend itself against the Tupamaros.

Specialists in Propaganda

The level of confusion has grown very deep and very serious. Yet we know it cannot be that terror wreaked on a civilian population by a revolutionary movement is liberation, while violence committed by a government responding to a guerrilla threat is repression. It cannot be that national liberation movements have the right to use violence against civilians, economies, societies and governments, and that those societies have no right to defend themselves—that violence conducted in the name of revolution is legitimate, while violence used by governments and societies to defend themselves against guerrillas is illegitimate. The distinction between terror used in defense of society and terror used to destroy society is really not so difficult. Many, however, have become confused by the semantics of totalitarianism, by the specialists in propaganda.

The liberation of Grenada provided, I believe, a particularly clear-cut example of the confusion surrounding the legitimate use of force, and not only of confusion inside the United Nations. Outside that

body, in some allied nations, extraordinary confusion was displayed as when a distinguished parliamentarian of a friendly government said:

> If the governments arrogate to themselves the right to change the governments of other sovereign states, there can be no peace in this world in perhaps the most dangerous age in which the human race has ever known. It is quite improper for Honorable Members to condemn, as we have, the violation of international law by the Soviet Union in its attack on Czechoslovakia and Afghanistan, if we do not apply the same standards to the United States' attack on Grenada two days ago.

I suggest that precisely what is at issue is applying the same standards, but applying them with realism and clarity.

Inside the United Nations, majorities in both the Security Council and the General Assembly rushed to condemn the acts of collective self-defense that liberated the inhabitants of Grenada from five days of absolute lawlessness—from five days of murder, of a four-day, 24-hour, shoot-on-sight curfew—in the hands of a group which boasted of the fact that it was not a government. That the action of the United States, the OECS, and Jamaica and Barbados was condemned—despite the clear and present danger to the United States' nationals; despite the fact that it was undertaken at the express request of the Governor-General of Grenada, which request was later confirmed by him; despite its basis in the collective defense provisions of the Treaty of the OECS; and in spite of the fact that it was undertaken to the manifest delight of the citizens of Grenada— that the condemnation took place under these circumstances is, I believe, the clearest recent example of the prevailing level of confusion. Unable to distinguish between force used to protect the innocent and force used to victimize, between force used to liberate and force used to enslave, successive majorities of the U.N. follow the principle of treating legitimacy as a function of will and power exercised in behalf of national liberation movements.

A Closed Society

There is one last affinity between terrorism and totalitarianism that I should like to mention. Both attempt to confuse as well as to terrorize. Solzhenitsyn, Orwell and others have emphasized that violence is used to maintain a system of lies, and lies are used to justify relations based on violence. . . .

Terrorists and totalitarians alike thrive on falsification and intimidation. Finding the courage to face the truth and speak about it is surely the first important step toward the defeat of those who would destroy our freedom and our world.

Jeane J. Kirkpatrick is a retired US ambassador to the United Nations.

"The Administration should propose increased resources for . . . the collection of counter-terrorist intelligence and the use of covert action against international terrorist groups."

Anti-Terrorist Actions Will Protect US Citizens

Samuel T. Francis

Despite an apparent decline in the number of terrorist incidents in the United States in 1983, public awareness of and concern over terrorism is probably greater today than at any time since the early 1970s. . . .

The Reagan Administration is trying to respond to the perceived or anticipated terrorist threat by instituting new security and counter-terrorist procedures and sponsoring legislation to address law enforcement problems of international terrorism. While critics contend that the terrorist threat is exaggerated and that some of the Administration proposals are unsuitable or ineffective, there can be no doubt that terrorism continues to take lives, cause injuries and damage to property, and destabilize politcal and social institutions in many parts of the world. The United States, moreover, as one of the world's most open and most powerful societies is highly vulnerable to terrorist violence and an attractive target for terrorists.

It is therefore reasonable for the U.S. government to take the internal and international terrorist threat seriously and to design measures to prevent terrorism and respond to terrorist attacks. While the White House has taken some steps in this direction, a clear and comprehensive policy is still needed. The Administration should move swiftly to formulate such a wide-ranging policy. Among other things, the Administration should propose increased resources for and easing restrictions on the collection of counter-terrorist intelligence and the use of covert action against international terrorist groups operating outside it but against U.S. targets. . . .

CIA Intelligence

There is an increasing appreciation within the Administration that intelligence on terrorist activities,

Samuel T. Francis, "Dealing with Terrorists: A Better US Policy Is Needed," Heritage Foundation *Backgrounder*, September 1984. Reprinted with permission.

groups, and supporters is the most effective means of anticipating and preventing terrorist acts. It also is recognized that there are serious deficiencies in U.S. Counter-Terrorist (CT) intelligence collection capabilities. In the 1970s, the U.S. intelligence community was seriously harmed by congressional investigations and press "exposes," and by the demoralization of the intelligence services following the cutbacks and dismissals in personnel and the prosecution of senior career intelligence officers such as Richard Helms of the CIA, and Mark Felt and Edward Miller of the FBI. Despite serious efforts by the Reagan Administration and some by Congress, the damage done in the 1970s is still felt today. Reported the *Wall Street Journal:*

> The CIA's failure to warn about bomb attacks against the U.S. Embassy and Marine headquarters in Beirut has many causes, including the loss of agents in Iran and in the Palestine Liberation Organization in the past several years. The U.S., for the moment, is dependent largely on other intelligence services, such as those of Israel, Jordan and Lebanon, which often lack detailed information from inside the terrorist groups. . . .

Covert Action

In a speech to the Trilateral Commission earlier this year, Secretary Shultz stated that:

> State-sponsored terrorism is really a form of warfare. Motivated by ideology and political hostility, it is a weapon of unconventional war against democratic societies, taking advantage of the openness of these societies . . . it is increasingly doubtful that a purely passive strategy can even begin to cope with the problem.

Shultz specifically mentioned "Iran, Syria, Libya, and North Korea" as supporters of terrorism. In later remarks before the Jonathan Institute conference, he added the Soviet Union to the list. Said Shultz: "The Soviets use terrorist groups for their own purposes, and their goal is always the same—to weaken liberal democracy and undermine world stability."

While Shultz's remarks on terrorism as a form of

war were clear, his suggestions for CT policies were less specific and more conventional. Among the measures he recommended were legislative responses, improved security and defenses, international cooperation, economic sanctions, better intelligence, and "appropriate preventive and preemptive actions." For the most part, these are all passive responses, and none was spelled out clearly.

"Intelligence on terrorist activities, groups, and supporters is the most effective means of anticipating and preventing terrorist acts."

Yet, while the concept of terrorism as a "form of war" waged covertly by hostile states is accurate, this is a view that has significantly different implications from the more conventional view of terrorism as crime. If the terrorist threat is seen as simply criminal, then it is primarily a law enforcement problem that can be met by passive measures carried out by law enforcement agencies. If, however, terrorism is a form of war or "unconventional war," as the Administration views it, then terrorism is a problem of national security; and not only law enforcement but also military and national security measures and agencies should be used against it.

Unconventional Warfare

One technique of unconventional warfare that has not been discussed much in terms of CT policy, but which follows logically from a view of terrorism as a form of war: covert action. This term, in recent years, has acquired a sinister connotation, suggesting assassinations, overthrow of governments, and other extralegal activities. Some "covert action," admittedly, includes such measures; typical covert activities, however, include propaganda, agents of influence, and nonviolent political, economic, or psychological warfare. "Covert action" is generally used to distinguish activities intended to influence other states or parties from intelligence collection. The principal reason for the clandestine nature of covert action is that if the U.S. government were to acknowledge it, that could thwart the purpose of the action. It is not to hide the action from responsible lawmakers or the public.

Covert action offers opportunities for CT measures abroad. Its principal purpose would be the disruption of terrorist organizations by striking at their internal unity and their ability to carry out acts of violence. While assassinations and preemptive strikes are coercive aspects of covert action, more effective (and less controversial) CT covert action would include:

1) dissemination of "black" (i.e., falsely attributed) propaganda to create dissension within terrorist groups, to discredit terrorist leaders and heroes and provoke defections, and perhaps to instigate internal, self-destructive violence among terrorist elements;

2) disruption of terrorist infrastructures by such means as neutralizing safehouses and sabotaging logistical systems;

3) use of disinformation against terrorists, terrorist supporters and sympathizers; public dissemination of identities of terrorist supporters and sympathizers to inhibit their operations.

Need for Secrecy

Varying forms of low-risk, low-level covert action against terrorists and their organizations could be crafted by intelligence services. For such measures to be effective, however, it is necessary for the U.S. to have reliable and detailed intelligence on targeted terrorist groups to anticipate accurately the results of such measures, to assure the security of covert operations, and to be able to deny credibly U.S. involvement in the action. The trouble now is that U.S. intelligence assets within terrorist groups have been reduced in recent years. Moreover, as the leak of the U.S. support for the mining of Nicaraguan harbors revealed, it is not certain that the U.S. can assure the clandestine nature of its covert action. Before such CT covert action can be implemented, therefore, reliable information and the secrecy of operations must be assured. . . .

Public and official concern over the terrorist threat to Americans, inside and outside the United States, has reached a serious level. This is understandable, considering the continuing attacks against American targets, the international collaboration among terrorist groups, and the state support for anti-American terrorism by hostile states. The Reagan Administration clearly shares this concern and has alerted and informed the American public, congressional leaders, and foreign allies of the terrorist threat. But while the Administration has taken concrete steps toward more effective counter-terrorist policies, it has not yet designed or implemented a comprehensive pro-active CT policy that conforms with its own understanding of terrorism as a "form of war." This clear policy is overdue.

Samuel T. Francis is legislative assistant for national security to senator John P. East (R-NC) and author of The Soviet Strategy of Terror.

"[Anti-terrorist strikes] will make a mockery of constitutional rights."

Anti-Terrorist Actions Threaten US Human Rights

The People

The Reagan administration's new policy against "terrorism" is supposed to protect our "values," our "institutions," and our "deeply held principles," according to various administration spokespersons. That policy will, in fact, further subvert the values, principles and institutions upon which both government by the people and civilization itself are based.

Few details of the policy have been made public. But the administration plans, in effect, to fight fire with fire.

In an April 3 speech, Secretary of State George Shultz denounced "state-supported terrorism" as a "form of warfare." He spoke of the need for an "active defense against terrorism" which would include "preventive or preemptive action against known terrorist groups."

Other reports indicate that the policy merely formalizes a number of concrete steps already secretly undertaken by the administration. These include:

• Increased spying at home and abroad by agencies such as the FBI, CIA and Defense Intelligence Agency (DIA);

• The setting up of FBI, CIA and Pentagon commando teams to attack alleged terrorists; and

• Sharp increases in funding and personnel for CIA clandestine operations.

In other words, the administration stands ready to fight "terrorism" by using the very tactics and actions usually associated with terrorism. Not only is such a policy hypocritical on its face, but it also rests on concepts and assumptions that are contrary to basic American political values and traditions and civilized ideas.

First of all, the basic concept of government by the

people requires that the people's business be conducted in public by their elected representatives. In no other way can the agencies of government be held accountable to those representatives and the representatives accountable to the people.

Like other so-called national security measures, however, the policy against "terrorism" is cloaked in secrecy. On the very day Shultz delivered the speech cited above, President Reagan signed National Security Decision Directive 138 which established the new policy.

Yet Shultz never mentioned the directive. It is still secret and is intended to remain so. Administration spokespersons have generally spoken only off the record and without attribution about many key points of the secret policy. Their intent is not to inform the public, but to intimidate their intended targets.

As public policy is being established in secret and without the informed consent of the American people, spy agencies such as the CIA, FBI and DIA are exercising an ever growing influence in government. Now those shadowy agencies will effectively decide who are the terrorists to be targeted and will carry out their missions in complete secrecy—at least until after the deed is done.

Imperial Presidency

Second, the policy furthers the trend toward what has been called "the imperial presidency." It concentrates powers in the hands of the president notwithstanding constitutional prohibitions.

National Security Decision Directive 138 establishes specific tactics for U.S. foreign policy and commits the United States to what is, by the administration's own reasoning, a "form of warfare." Yet this document was not enacted by Congress but established by presidential decree.

In fact, in his April 3 speech, Shultz specifically criticized congressional restrictions on supposed presidential powers. The U.S. Constitution clearly

The People, "'Antiterrorist' Campaign a Threat to Basic Rights," May 12, 1984. Reprinted with permission.

delegates to Congress the power to declare war. Yet Shultz found the War Power Act, which unconstitutionally cedes much of that power to the president, unduly restrictive.

"Our commander in chief is locked in battle at home at the same time he is trying to act effectively abroad," Shultz said. "Micromanagement by a committee of 535 independent-minded individuals is a grossly inefficient and ineffective way to run any important enterprise."

That is one argument often advanced in favor of dictatorship—efficiency and effectiveness. Policy can be decided upon and implemented rapidly if determined by the will of one person.

That sort of autocracy, however, is exactly what was supposed to be prevented by the numerous checks and balances written into the U.S. Constitution. Its authors had seen the tyranny of George III and his ministers and were determined to prevent the establishment of such an oppressive government over the new republic.

Subverting Justice

Third, the idea of preemptive or retaliatory strikes against alleged terrorists violates two cardinal principles of justice—that one is presumed innocent until proven guilty and that no one judge one's own case. Under the administration's policy, spy agencies will act as prosecutor, judge, jury and executioner, determining who is allegedly to blame for terrorism and administering summary punishment.

"There will be no rule of law, no due process, no appeal, just attacks by armed commandos."

Antiterrorist strikes will occur at home and abroad. At home, they will make a mockery of constitutional rights. There will be no rule of law, no due process, no appeal, just attacks by armed commandos.

Abroad, U.S. commandos will ignore international borders in order to strike at what is considered a terrorist threat. They will enforce U.S. claims to act anywhere in any way on its own so to defend its "security" interests.

Moreover, the history of the spy agencies makes it clear that "terrorism" is not their primary target—at home or abroad. It is a matter of record that such agencies acted to disrupt and sometimes violently repress the antiwar, civil rights movements in the 1960s and early 1970s.

Abroad, they engaged in such actions as overthrowing governments in Iran, Guatemala and Chile, the torture and execution of peasants in Vietnam, assassinations and attempted assassinations of political leaders, and other dirty deeds intended to install or prop up repressive pro-U.S. regimes.

In view of the fact that the government has previously defined as "terrorist" peaceful and legal political organizations in the United States and national liberation movements abroad, the present danger cannot be overemphasized. It is no secret that the spy agencies are already engaged in infiltrating and disrupting the disarmament movement at home and trying to overthrow the government of Nicaragua abroad.

In accepting this policy with little protest, the present ruling class has made it clear that it is ready to sacrifice the values and ideals it still professes to uphold in an effort to preserve its rule and wealth. It readily places considerations of power before those of principle.

Such a ruling class is unfit to govern. Its system can no longer serve society's interests nor preserve the values and principles upon which civilization depends. To serve the social interest and uphold the principles of democracy and civilization requires sweeping away the capitalist system and its ruling class.

The People *is a daily newspaper of the Socialist Labor Party.*

"The United States and its allies are continually improving their ability to identify specific terrorist threats and prevent attacks."

viewpoint**105**

Terrorism Is Controllable

Noel C. Koch

During the past decade, terrorist acts directed against U.S. government officials and installations abroad have averaged one every 17 days, and in countries where the American military constitutes a high profile presence, our men in uniform have become prime terrorist targets.

Terrorist operations are becoming bolder and bloodier. According to one calculation, 80 percent of all terrorist attacks during the early 1970s were directed against property rather than people. By the 1980s, the balance had shifted, with approximately half of all operations targeted against personnel. Since the 1970s, fatal incidents have increased by roughly 20 percent per year.

In the aftermath of the Oct. 23, 1983, bombing of the Marine battalion landing team's quarters in Beirut, state supported terrorism became a major focus of public concern. In fact, the involvement of other governments in training, supplying, and financing terrorism has been a feature of this activity for years. The only real change is the increased involvement of states unskilled at, or indifferent to, the business of maintaining deniability.

According to recent estimates, roughly 70 attacks in 1983 alone can be traced to state-supported terrorism. The types of assistance offered terrorist groups include safehaven, documentation, communications, propaganda and logistical support—including use of the diplomatic pouch. In some cases, governments have selected the target and provided operational guidance and vulnerability data on the prospective victim. Iran, Libya, Syria, and North Korea are the most blatant practitioners of this form of warfare.

Dual-Track Policy

Other countries, such as the Soviet Union, Cuba, and Nicaragua, pursue a dual-track policy. They take greater care to conceal their involvement with terrorists to afford themselves an element of plausible denial and, thereby, maintain maximum flexibility in the diplomatic arena. They provide covert support to terrorist groups while concurrently espousing peaceful coexistence and non-intervention. Their approach is more sophisticated, divisive, and ultimately more difficult to counter. Many of their target audiences—whether through ideological affinity or political naivete—choose to accept their assurances of non-complicity and ignore the hard evidence provided by defectors, captured subversives, and Western intelligence services. The public may be outraged at the terrorist act but—without the smoking gun—is slow to condemn the countries that made the deed possible.

State-supported terrorism forces international conflict into a grey area not readily accommodated by existing conventions and international law. Put another way, it engenders an international lawlessness which aims at the heart of that body of custom and convention which sustains orderly relations between nations. The only beneficiary of this consequence is the world's principal expansionist power.

The U.S. response to international terrorism is multifaceted. One of the most important steps has also been among the most difficult—simply bringing the American people to a full appreciation of the threat we face and to understand that there are no fast, easy solutions to the threat.

Legislative Initiatives

The administration proposed a series of legislative initiatives for confronting terrorism, and most of these have passed the Congress. These include the payment of substantial rewards for significant terrorist intelligence, legislation implementing existing international anti-terrorism agreements, and supplemental funding to provide enhanced security

Noel C. Koch, "Terrorism: The Undeclared War," *Defense*, March 1985.

for our installations overseas. Congress has also approved a Department of State-sponsored anti-terrorism program for foreign governments, which provides terrorist incident management training in the United States for foreign civil officials.

The United States and its allies are continually improving their ability to identify specific terrorist threats and prevent attacks through increased cooperation and the sharing of sensitive intelligence data. Additional funding has been provided U.S. intelligence agencies to enhance their collection and analytical capabilities. Significant personnel and material resources have been committed to this effort.

"The Department of Defense has a very broad involvement in the effort to combat terrorism."

The Department of Defense has a very broad involvement in the effort to combat terrorism, beginning with its concern for protecting U.S. military personnel and dependents overseas. We have increased emphasis on training, awareness, and security programs to protect our personnel and facilities from terrorist attacks, while improving our ability to detect threats and identify those responsible for acts which threaten our security. Programs are based on a balance among the threat, degree of protection required, mission requirements, manpower available, and fiscal constraints.

Defense Training

Training in defense against terrorism has been integrated into most service school curricula, mobile training teams are being used to provide training to overseas commands, and personnel assigned to areas vulnerable to terrorist attack are receiving specialized briefings on the threat and security precautions available to counter the threat. Extensive reviews of our security procedures have been conducted and additional physical security measures instituted to protect our forces, dependents, and facilities.

The Department of Defense also maintains operational elements capable of resolving by force terrorist incidents of duration. As the threat moves away from incidents of this nature, new skills and methodologies are being developed to cope with it.

The targets of terrorism are not American lives and property. The real targets are the fundamental values of the Western democracies.

It is this feature of terrorism that constitutes its principal strength. Nietzsche said that it is necessary when fighting monsters to avoid becoming a monster. Time will tell whether terrorist assaults on the United States seriously erode our credibility as a great power

and, if so, whether that erosion will have long term implications or whether, in the long term, we will be seen as having been patient in the face of provocation and confident enough of our power to be prudent in its exercise. What is certain is that if in order to fight terrorism we abandon the moral values upon which our society rests and from which it derives the very strength that brings us under attack, then we will indeed risk our credibility as a great power and will concede to terrorism the victory it seeks.

Unsuccessful Terrorism

It is helpful to recognize that a successful terrorist action doesn't consist in kidnapping, hijacking or killing people, but rather in achieving some larger goal thereby. By this criterion, contemporary terrorism has enjoyed relatively limited success, and the trend for these successes is down, not up.

With so much attention being paid to terrorism and so much frustration evinced over a seeming inability to stop it, it is difficult to recognize the evidence that those who practice terrorism do not have it all their own way.

To take a case in point, there was a time when Kuwait was a favored haven for terrorists who could count on at least passive assistance in whatever they happened to be doing—usually hijacking an aircraft. Yet in the last year, Kuwait has arrested, tried, convicted, and sentenced terrorists involved in bombing the U.S. and French Embassies there and in December bravely stood up to a brutal terrorist hijacking and refused to make concessions to end it.

Kuwait did this with the support and encouragement of neighbors who had, themselves, on other occasions been intimidated into acquiescing in terrorist activities. In the end, the December hijacking was a defeat for terrorism.

Terrorism sought to destroy Israel's citrus export market. It failed. It sought to deter tourists from flying to Israel. Again, it failed.

Patient Resistance

The Red Brigades subjected Italy to a reign of terror stretching over nearly two decades and aimed at nothing less than destroying the pluralistic system of government in Italy. The effort has served only to further strengthen Italy. The stubborn resistance of the Italians to the terrorist menace is a record of patience, courage, and self-confidence that should serve to demonstrate the power of a free people certain of their bedrock convictions.

Turkey has withstood egregious assault and crushed terrorism within its borders without crushing its people's efforts to make representative government work.

England and West Germany have demonstrated that nations need not choose between compromising with terrorism and compromising their principles.

So has the United States. Terrorism has not

deterred our support for our friends, our opposition to our adversaries, our quest for a just peace in the Middle East, our aid to the democratically elected government of El Salvador and other friends in Latin America, our strong relations with Egypt, the Sudan, and Chad, nor the maintenance of a strong NATO Alliance.

Victorious Year

By all calculations, 1984 was to have been a year of frightful vulnerability for the United States. We had a World's Fair, two national political conventions, an international Olympics, and a presidential election. Because of a strong intergovernmental effort, and particularly that professionalism which we take for granted from the Federal Bureau of Investigation, these events concluded peacefully. These were victories.

For those who find cold comfort in these "victories" as they are held next to headlines recording the deaths of innocent Americans, it may be helpful to look at the world through the terrorists' eyes. As revolting as the exercise may seem, it is necessary to submit to it in order to "know your enemy." As perverse as it may seem, the terrorist is committed to an objective, a vision, even an "ideal," larger than his own glorious demise.

Object of Revulsion

The terrorist looks out on a world which, not universally, but in many quarters, romanticized him and gave him a grudging respect; which often sympathized with his motives, if not his deeds; which allowed him a measure of tolerance, if not acceptance. Today, he is an object of revulsion.

The terrorist enjoyed some early successes: Communiques conveying grievances blared through the international media, ransoms were paid, colleagues were released from prison. Today, it doesn't happen; the communique is a bargaining chip, and nobody cares about the grievance.

Drama was the soul of terrorism and required the color and suspense of hostages barricaded in mortal danger. Entebbe, Mogadishu, Princessgate, Bangkok, and a host of lesser known rescues ended the drama.

This has pushed the threat to bombs and assassinations and, these having quickly acquired a fatal ordinariness, to bigger bombs. But without the drama, these became acts of violence, the senselessness of which its most abject apologists can no longer deny.

Contemporary terrorism began in czarist Russia, its intellectual engine nihilism, its object anarchy. It borrowed from the assumption that regicide could bring down more than a man, that it could change or destroy the oppressive structure upon which he rested. History has not been unkind to this assumption. Indeed, we have seen the spiritual heirs of the concept institutionalize murder as an instrument of state policy. The consolidation of Soviet power in eastern Europe was advanced through the murders of nationalist leaders. Nor has the technique lost its attraction today, and we may expect to see further efforts to strike down living symbols of all that terrorism hates. Thus, the attack on Pope John Paul, the plot to kill Lech Walesa, the murder of Anwar Sadat, the murders of members of the Republic of Korea's cabinet in an effort to kill President Chon Do Won, the murder of Indira Gandhi, the murder of Father Popieluszko, and the attempt to kill Prime Minister Margaret Thatcher.

Terrorists Are Losers

So it is not accidental that so many murders or attempts to murder present-day authority figures are the products of state-supported terrorism. But today what is repugnant and oppressive to the sponsors of terrorism has no roots in the arbitrary tyrannies of 18th and 19th century Russia and Europe, but rather is human freedom itself, and murder cannot deter a people's will to be free. So the sponsors of international terrorism are on a losing wicket. They seek to achieve encouraging successes; barring these, they must achieve what they can before their human resources dry up. And, the further they proceed, the more they flirt with the prospect of war on other than terms of their own choosing.

"Contemporary terrorism has enjoyed relatively limited success, and the trend for these successes is down, not up."

Like a book held to the nose, terrorism is difficult to read, and the vague impression of the print is black. Perspective is required, and this is the purpose of efforts to inform Americans fully of the threat and the unique problems in confronting it. . . .

An imperfect awareness of our own history obscures the fact that we have weathered in our own past worse experiences with terrorism than confront us today. An imperfect reading of the Western democracies had led others, from time to time, to confuse forebearance with fragility and humanistic values with vulnerability.

In the nature of the present problem, terrorist acts are always well known, while our own successes are almost always silent. They will almost always continue to be. But we have not defaulted, we are not helpless, and we have no doubt, as terrorism can have no doubt, of the outcome.

Noel C. Koch is principal deputy, assistant Secretary of Defense for International Security Affairs.

Terrorism Is Uncontrollable

Glenn Garvin

Think of it as a jigsaw puzzle, the pieces dark, jagged, and often indistinct: Acrid smoke curling around the Capitol dome on a cold December night; an Islamic cleric, crumpled in the foyer of his suburban Detroit home, clutching frantically at his face to stop the bleeding from a crooked row of 9mm bullet holes; or the bewildered look of an Alexandria storage company worker as he peers into a shed at 95 precisely-stacked sticks of a high explosive.

When you snap enough of the pieces together, there's a bigger picture—a frightening one. Terrorism has come to America.

It is a chilling word, an ugly word. It seems out of place here. It is a European word, or a Middle Eastern word—a word for countries where tiny, fanatic sects of unfamiliar religions and cryptic political groups spin out nihilistic fantasies. But it is a word that we will learn to use more easily here. Jet airplanes and satellite communications and scientific developments have helped the terrorist hone and craft his centuries-old black art into modern, technological shapes. And they have brought him to our door.

Scarcely a week goes by without word of some new chapter in the American terrorist handbook. New-Left bombers practice a lethal form of urban renewal on New York corporate skyscrapers. Pro-life fanatics leave ironic calling cards, in the form of pipe bombs, at abortion clinics. Radical Puerto Rican nationalists blow up police stations and policemen. Disgruntled Cuban exiles lob a missile at Castro's U.N. mission.

Sometimes it is a continuation of an old feud from another time, another place, and the United States is little more than this week's stage. Armenian gunmen cut down Turkish diplomats in revenge for a massacre that took place seven decades ago and 5,000 miles away. Rival Islamic groups take target practice on one another in holy wars that have lasted centuries, the origins long since forgotten even by some of the participants.

Other incidents are peculiarly 20th century American, like a wave of 24 pipe-bombings that plagued the Midwest this spring, committed by a man who claimed he acted on behalf of the "North Central Gay Strike Force."

Some terrorists find support from other countries—for instance, from Cuba, which has trained some New Leftists and Puerto Rican nationalists in the fine art of bomb building; from Libya, which has occasionally hired freelance hitmen to silence its exiled critics; or from Chile, which has lent technical aid to anti-Castro Cubans in the United States.

Sometimes support for terrorism comes from even stranger sources. Miami Herald reporters once held a bake sale in their newsroom to raise money for the Irish Republican Army (IRA). And, until recently, a North Carolina congressman was employing on his staff a member of the John Brown Anti-Klan Committee, which most law enforcement officials regard as a front group for the Weather Underground and other New Left terrorist organizations. . . .

"Don't be misled by the number of incidents," says Terrell Arnold, the State Department's antiterrorist coordinator. "To be sure, since 1979 the number of incidents individually have been more violent. Terrorist groups have targeted in a more indiscriminate manner. The devices have become larger and more destructive."

Terrorist Techniques

The kind of thing Mr. Arnold is talking about has been more readily apparent overseas—in the Islamic suicide bombing of the U.S. Embassy in Beirut, Lebanon, which killed 63, or the IRA's Christmas bombing of a London department store that took five lives and injured 91. In these incidents, bombs were

Glenn Garvin, "America Is in Their Gunsights," *The Washington Times*, June 24, 1985. Reprinted with permission.

detonated in places where they would strike not only the intended targets, but dozens of bystanders who had nothing to do with the bombers' political grievance.

But there are indications that "loose" targeting may become a habit in the United States as well. Late last year the FBI foiled an attempt by a pro-Khomeini Iranian group to plant a bomb in a theater where some anti-Khomeini Iranian entertainers were performing. Loss of life would easily have been in the dozens.

"The very essence of terrorism is that it's hard to get at, hard to retaliate against, hard to defend against."

And the bomb that exploded at the Capitol on a Monday night [in December 1983], doing $1 million worth of damage, went off just outside the Senate chambers at a time when the Senators had expected to be in session. They weren't. But if they had been . . . It's a thought that makes the counterterror community shudder. The bomb was planted inside a hinged window box across from the Republican cloakroom.

"There's a glass wall in there," says Joel Lisker, chief counsel to the Senate subcommittee on security and terrorism. "I saw the cloakroom afterwards—the glass was just like shrapnel, punching great big holes in the wall. If those guys had been in there watching Monday night football, as they would have been, it would have just been slaughter."

The Capitol bombing sent a ripple of fear through much of the country—Texas ended 24-hour access to its capitol building, and several other states tightened security—but nowhere have the effects been felt more keenly than in Washington, which already had a collective case of the jitters.

Search for Publicity

"If you want to strike a blow against the United States of America, you don't go to Des Moines, Iowa, and blow up a cow," noted a Washington policeman last year. Not when a city full of highly visible monuments and government institutions is available.

Overnight, concrete barriers, thinly disguised as planters, appeared at the Capitol, the White House, and the State Department. The Pentagon barricaded its underground traffic tunnels. Metal detectors went up all over the city.

But how can you stop one determined terrorist? An Israeli tourist evaded all security precautions last fall and got into the House visitors' gallery in the Capitol with a bomb strapped to his waist. The only thing that prevented an enormous loss of life was the fact that he had miswired the bomb and it didn't go off.

Some people believe there was another, even more terrifying, narrow miss in September 1981. A Palestinian activist named Abdul-Hafiz Mohammed Nassar bought 100 pounds of a high explosive called Kinepak—enough to blow down a city block—in Arizona, then drove to Washington. He arrived on Sept. 8, one day before Israeli Prime Minister Menachem Begin was scheduled to visit the White House. And that afternoon, Nassar got a parking ticket on 17th Street NW—less than two blocks from the White House.

Was he planning to blow up the White House? Nassar, who was caught and pleaded guilty to federal explosives charges, says no—that the explosive was intended for shipment to the Middle East. The FBI believes him. But there is one other curious detail about this case.

Nassar's actions came to light in May 1982, when workers at a self-storage company in Alexandria cut a lock off a shed that he had rented while he was in Washington. The rent was overdue, and the company intended to sell whatever was inside. They found 95 sticks of the explosive Kinepak, along with 11 blasting caps and four two-way radios that could be used to detonate the explosive by remote control.

Deadlier than Dynamite

And here is the thing that bothers some people. Kinepak is a "binary" explosive, consisting of two ingredients that have to be mixed before it will explode. Before they are mixed, it's as harmless as Silly Putty; afterwards, it's ready to blow, deadlier than dynamite. When the two ingredients are mixed, the Kinepak turns a bright pink to signal danger.

When the employees at the storage company broke into the locker, the Kinepak was bright pink. If Nassar intended to ship it overseas, why would he prepare it for detonation?

Terror-thinkers worry about bombs. They should: 98,000 pounds of explosives have been stolen in the United States during the past two years.

They do not worry very much about terrorists' obtaining a nuclear device. The consensus is that the materials and the technical know-how would be too hard to obtain. Far more probable, the experts say, is a biological or chemical attack. "There's lots of stuff in terrorist literature about biochemical attacks, although I haven't seen it happen yet," says Robert Kupperman, a Pentagon consultant and a senior associate at the Georgetown Center for Strategic and International Studies (CSIS).

Failed Attempts

Actually, attempts have been made, but so far they have failed. Half a dozen or so times in the 1970s, Italian terrorists tried to poison city water supplies. In 1973 a Yugoslavian-born terrorist sent toxic chemicals through the mail to Supreme Court Justice Thurgood Marshall. A group in Chicago dumped typhoid bacillus into a reservoir—it died.

But a successful biochemical attack would be simple—"frighteningly simple," in the words of the Naval War College Review.

"Terrorists using biological agents could disperse them among bulk food suppliers, e.g. at a central market, a large-scale catering operation, or even a single supermarket," the review observed. "Chemical agents could be effective if introduced into an air handling system in a small office building, or dispersed, say, from an ice cream cart standing amidst thousands of people in a large auditorium."

Obtaining the germs themselves is probably the easiest part. There is a company in Rockville that sells the bacillus that produces botulism toxin for $34 a shot. The company even has a toll-free number for quick service. Mr. Kupperman estimates that an attack with biological agents could easily kill hundreds of people; with chemical agents, tens of thousands. . . .

History of Terror

Terrorism is nothing new, even in the United States. "It's as American as apple pie," says Yonah Alexander of CSIS. The Capitol was first bombed in 1915—by a Harvard professor who thought the Wilson administration was conniving against Germany. In the years before World War I, anarchists routinely set off bombs and shot at political figures (and even killed President William McKinley). Racial terror by whites against blacks was common in the South as recently as 20 years ago.

Terrorism in the United States goes clear back to the Boston Tea Party, and in the rest of the world at least to the 11th century, when the notorious Hasan Sabah fed his fundamentalist Moslem men hashish and sent them out from his castle in northern Iran to kill political enemies. It was a fabulously successful strategy that kept Hasan and his heirs in power for 200 years.

Hasan left us both a new word ("hashashin," since corrupted to "assassin") and a legacy of political terror that has drawn frightening new vigor from modern technology. "What's new in international terrorism," says Mr. Kupperman, "is jet aircraft—the ability to go from place to place very quickly; satellite communications, which make it easy to plan, coordinate, and communicate; support states; and a media that's willing to get whipped up by them."

All those factors have drawn terrorists inexorably to the United States. An Armenian terrorist can pick up a phone and talk to comrades in Europe and the Middle East for help in picking a target; gun down a Turkish diplomat in Los Angeles, guaranteeing worldwide publicity generated by the huge American media; and then get on a plane and leave the state, or even the country, in a matter of hours.

The global impact of American news media is a key attraction for terrorists, who may have no grudge at all against the United States. "They don't call the police agencies after they've done something. They call the news agencies," Mr. Revell said. "That obviously is their purpose—to get out the message."

International Ties

There is another variety of terrorist being drawn to the United States—one that acts with the sponsorship of another country. In the last 20 years, some countries have discovered that terrorists are less expensive and more versatile than armies. The second most-quoted cliche among terror-thinkers: Terrorism is warfare on the cheap.

"It's an easy weapon, inexpensive, easy to activate and difficult to counter," says Yonah Alexander, "especially when you use proxies." Adds his CSIS colleague Robert Kupperman, "One of the beauties of terrorism, using proxies, is that one can occasion the opportunity of plausible deniability. That is, tell the target, 'Go prove it!'"

State-supported terrorism first began cropping up about 20 years ago, when Fidel Castro sent Che Guevara abroad to foment revolution throughout Latin America. European terrorists have long had training and support from Marxist-Leninist governments, particularly the Soviet bloc. But during the last five years, state-supported terrorism has grown even more ominous, with terrorist groups acting as direct agents of other countries.

"The potential for death and destruction is almost unlimited."

"I think the Iranians' ability to take the hostages, and our inability to do anything about that—worse yet, the busted rescue operation—gave a lot of nations the idea that they could do this," says Mr. Kupperman. Practically everyone who studies terrorism agrees that the bombings of the U.S. Embassy and Marine barracks in Beirut, just to name two prominent examples, were committed by an Islamic terrorist group acting on behalf of Iran or Syria. But, to a man, they agree that "we don't have the kind of evidence that would stand up in court."

And retaliation is nearly impossible. "The very essence of terrorism is that it's hard to get at, hard to retaliate against, hard to defend against," says Rand Corporation analyst Conrad Kellen. The Reagan administration, which has endorsed the idea of retaliatory strikes, has discovered the practical difficulties of carrying them out. The administration is certain that the bombings of the U.S. Embassy and the Marine barracks in Beirut last year were carried out by an Islamic fundamentalist group—but where do you find them? How do you strike back?

Islamic Holy War

Besides the two Beirut bombings, the group known as Islamic Holy War has been blamed for last year's bombing of the U.S. Embassy in Kuwait. Total death toll: 378. In each case, the terrorists simply drove a vehicle through whatever defenses were around the building and detonated a huge bomb that killed them, along with all the other victims.

Islamic Holy War is made up of radical members of the Shi'ite sect of the Moslem religion. The Shi'ites—who were, ironically, close allies of old Hasan Sabbah—may pose the single most troubling development in the world of terrorism. Their willingness—some would say eagerness—to die for the cause renders many of the standard protections against terrorism useless. "How can you stop something like that?" says Joel Lisker. The answer is simple: You can't.

"The global impact of American news media is a key attraction for terrorists."

The Shi'ites have put their services at the disposal of a number of nations and causes in the Middle East, notably Iran and Syria, further complicating the international terrorist marketplace. "The Soviets had a near monopoly for a while, but I think it's gotten out of their hands now," says Mr. Kupperman.

"Some people tend to deal with these things in a simplistic way," agrees Buck Revell. "The KGB doesn't direct every incident of terrorism in the Middle East. The empirical evidence just doesn't support that.

"Certainly they're going to take advantage of it. Certainly they're going to aid everybody in sympathy with their ideology. All these things are true, but they don't add up to a great big building in the Kremlin where everything is mapped out."

But, from a practical standpoint, the involvement of the Soviets is irrelevant. State-supported terrorists, no matter who sponsors them, have access to more money, better equipment and more destructive technology. Coupled with the emergence of the fanatic Shi'ites, willing to launch kamikaze-style attacks that will end in certain death for the attackers, the potential for death and destruction is almost unlimited.

"You're dealing with a war, and it's not seen as a war," warns Mr. Alexander. "That's the problem. It's not a war where you deploy divisions. All the missiles and the other weapons of the United States are worthless in this war."

Glenn Garvin is a reporter with The Washington Times.

"The stakes are too high, the alternative too deadly, for the option of rapprochement to be discarded."

The US Should Seek Rapprochement with Terrorist States

Robin Wright

Shortly after American hostages were taken at the United States Embassy in Tehran in 1979, President Jimmy Carter summoned University of Virginia Prof. R. K. Ramazani, America's leading expert on Iranian foreign policy, to a meeting in the Oval Office. Repeatedly Carter stressed that the United States was not in conflict with Islam, only the Iranians, Ramazani recalled later.

Carter was right in recognizing the problem, but events have proved that separating the two is not quite so easy. In Islam, politics and religion are inseparable. And in the late 20th century, the Islamic fundamentalism preached from Iran has become the most potent force for discontent and revolution throughout the Middle East.

That force is behind the hijacking of TWA 847, as well as the earlier bombings of the Marine compound, two U.S. embassies in Beirut and the American mission in Kuwait over the past 26 months. American diplomats throughout the region now work behind tank traps and machine gun emplacements in diplomatic fortresses. U.S. citizens often live like recluses.

Five months after the 1983 Marine bombing, Dr. Marvin Zonis, director of the Middle East Institute at the University of Chicago, spoke at a State Department seminar on "The Psychological Roots of Shiite Terrorism." "The message from Iran—no matter how bizarre or trivial it sounds on first, second, fourth or 39th hearing—is in my opinion the single most impressive political ideology which has been proposed in the 20th century since the Bolshevik revolution," he said. "This powerful message will be with us for a very long time, no matter what happens to Ayatollah Khomeini."

The killing of a passenger on the TWA plane by

Shiite fanatics was just one of many indications that resolution of the immediate hijacking ordeal will not mean the end of the U.S. conflict with Shiite militants in Lebanon or elsewhere.

A Trying Conflict

In effect, the United States is engaged in a war, perhaps the most trying and unconventional conflict it has ever faced. The opposition is amorphous and diffuse, often without identifiable leaders, members or headquarters.

It is tempting to want to strike back, to confront attackers with conventional military force. But the nature of this war is such that it is not against a state or an area with borders, against which it would be easy to launch air strikes or land assaults. The foe is a religious movement whose foot soldiers are not confined to a single country or sect.

Yet a state—Iran—is the locus of the acts that are so disturbing to the United States. In 1983, the Reagan administration officially labeled Iran a primary sponsor of state-supported terrorism. It is more accurate to call it state-inspired, for the Islamic Republic's main role is as a model and catalyst.

Beyond the theological and intellectual ties, Shiite fanatics in Lebanon, and elsewhere, have visible links with Iran. Several leading Lebanese mullahs travel regularly to Tehran. The Iranian Revolutionary Guards stationed in Lebanon's eastern Bekaa valley since 1982 have provided material and political support for the extremist factions. Dozens of young fighters from different groups have received military training at camps scattered throughout Iran. Among them is the military chief of Lebanon's Amal movement, a youth who between 1979 and 1982 hijacked six planes traveling to or from Libya.

Yet neither the Iranian revolution nor the subsequent war would have happened if there had not been deep-seated antagonism toward the United States. Islamic fundamentalists feel they have not

Robin Wright: "The Terrorism Won't End Till We Come to Terms with Iran," *The Washington Post National Weekly Edition*, July 8, 1985. Reprinted with the author's permission.

initiated the trouble, but have responded to an opponent that they feel started it. Their extremism is not for love of violence. Their revolution is against what they feel is foreign domination and encroachment in every aspect of their lives—symbolized most often by the United States.

One point of consensus among the diverse Shiite groups, who often disagree with each other on other major issues and tactics, is that they see themselves as having lived under the heel of the United States for 40 years—since America became the main influence in the Middle East.

"During the rapprochement process, neither side need succumb or lose face."

Among the most often cited American "offenses" against Moslem lands and peoples: CIA assistance to Shah Mohammed Reza Pahlavi in the 1953 overthrow of a nationalist movement led by Prime Minister Mohammed Mossadegh, who had been successfully undermining the royal family's then fragile position.

Nationalists and Shiite fundamentalists came to share a resentment of what they saw as the Shah's servile attitude toward the U.S.

The United States is criticized by militants for trying in the 1960s to manipulate coups in Syria and backing a corrupt king in Libya. In the 1980s, American troops and warships went on the offensive for the first time since Vietnam—against Muslims. The use of American firepower was not to protect endangered American lives but to protect a minority government in Lebanon.

US Terrorist Activities

The United States was most recently linked indirectly to a bomb that went off last March near the home of one of Lebanon's most militant Shiite clerics, killing more than 80, although not the cleric. The bombers reportedly had ties to a group being trained by the CIA.

The long record of fears and suspicions about U.S. intentions in the region was reflected in the manifesto of Lebanon's Hizbollah, or Party of God, released a month later: "Imam Khomeini, the leader, has repeatedly stressed that America is the reason for all our catastrophes and the source of all malice. By fighting it, we are only exercising our legitimate right to defend our Islam and the dignity of our nation. We have opted for religion, freedom and dignity over humiliation and constant submission to America and its allies."

A member of Hizbollah said in an interview shortly after the bombing of the second U.S. Embassy annex in Beirut last September: "We aren't against the American people. We are against oppression and injustice. The fire of Islam will burn those who are responsible for these practices [against Islam]. We have been dominated by the U.S. government and others for too long."

U.S. policy in the Middle East, which emphasizes the security of Israel, is also a major cause of the militants' wrath. But the militants' reaction to the United States is probably linked more to American policy on other Islamic issues over the past 40 years than to U.S. positions on the Arab-Israeli dispute.

Indeed, for more than a month before the TWA hijacking, Shiite militiamen were engaged in bloody clashes with Palestinians. The Shiites desire the return of historic Jerusalem to Moslem control primarily because it contains the third holiest site in Islam and less because the Palestinians want a homeland. Settlement of the Palestinian question would probably not end the fundamentalists' anti-American campaign.

Three Policy Options

Yet the hijacking of TWA 847 could serve as a turning point for U.S. policy to end a conflict that is taking a mounting toll in American lives. But the Reagan administration must use extreme caution in analyzing which of three main policy options it adopts: force, sanctions or rapprochement. Otherwise, the U.S. may face an escalation that will make the recent wave of bombings, kidnappings and hijackings seem small-scale by comparison.

Unfortunately, since the attacks began, U.S. policy makers have seen only the violence in the extreme fundamentalist movement without understanding its political roots or its social importance. And the Reagan administration seems intent on sending a message to the militants and their sponsors by using force, probably a quick, supposedly surgical strike after the hijacking is resolved.

What has made Iran such a frustrating conundrum to American policy makers is the perception that it acts on the basis of passion rather than thoughtful policy. Ironically, the Reagan administration may be in grave danger of succumbing to the same emotionalism that it sees in the fundamentalists.

But the use of force, the first policy option, is likely to be catastrophic in the long run for the United States, for three reasons. First, contrary to public hopes that it will cripple or discourage the movement, the use of force against the Shiite militants would only fuel their resentment and commitment, providing new reasons for seeking revenge against the "Great Satan," as well as creating an even more hostile, anti-American atmosphere, thereby attracting new recruits.

Shiite Extremists

The Shiite extremist has become a Hydra: kill one and two appear in his place. The movements in general have simply become too big to stop by cleaning out a training camp or two, especially with the growth over the past 18 months of a large, politicized body of Shiites, who agree with the zealots' motives and goals, if not their tactics.

As Israel's tragic experience in Lebanon showed, an "eye for an eye" policy only escalates the cycle of violence into a long-term confrontation. The Shiite militants are truly prepared to die in acts that they do not view as terrorism but as noble deeds against perceived aggressors in defense of their faith and independence.

The dimensions of the problem are reflected in attempts to pinpoint the groups or individuals responsible. Washington officials last year charged that the Party of God was responsible for the second embassy bombing, which elicited a bitter snicker from an American diplomat on the ground in Lebanon. "That doesn't tell us anything," he said. "Every Shiite in Lebanon is now Hizbollah"—a statement that was only a slight exaggeration.

A Terrorist Blessing

The name of Sheikh Mohammed Hussein Fadlallah, the cleric whose neighborhood was bombed last March, keeps appearing in relation to various acts, including charges that he provided or blessed the suicide drivers who bombed the Marine compound. Heated debate still rages over his involvement, but even if the allegation were true, proving it would be difficult, since he has repeatedly and publicly condemned hijackings, kidnappings and bombings as "un-Islamic" and his headquarters is a mosque.

Unlike most other insurgency movements, the Shiites have often used legitimate institutions as centers of operations. "You simply can't raid a mosque or penetrate a cell centered around an Islamic social center," says a Gulf state intelligence officer. "And even if you did, you would probably be unable to find anything incriminating beyond a copy of the Koran."

Second, the use of force would also endanger our allies, especially the moderate Muslims who already have problems with fundamentalists at home, in part because of their ties to the United States. Although the fundamentalist campaign is unlikely to bring down other Muslim governments, it can force them through continuing intimidation and terror to accept their extremist tenets.

Third, the use of force is not foolproof. It carries the danger of defeat that could in turn lead to intervention by the Soviets or others. The basis of the conflict is both political and religious, impervious to the use of force.

The second policy option is economic sanctions, which are unlikely to work because of Iran's oil.

Iran's revolution has proved defiantly durable, surviving the drain of earlier sanctions, the challenge from opposition groups, both right and left, the trauma of almost five years of war and the isolation

and hostility incurred because of its policies. The reality is that many Iranians, who already are living with meat and petrol rationing, appear to be prepared to endure further hardships to protect their Islamic form of government.

High Vulnerability

American vulnerability, on the other hand, has never been greater. More than 55,000 American diplomats and federal civilian employees live abroad in 10,000 different facilities, in addition to tens of thousands of American military personnel at bases around the world. The State Department unofficially estimates that more than 1.7 million American civilians live overseas. Merely tightening security, discouraging the use of certain international airports or spending millions to improve diplomatic installations is not going to prevent further attacks.

To end the Shiites' war against the United States, the Reagan administration has no alternative but to defuse the tension with Iran, which has led Islam to its first total "victory" of this century. Most serious militants follow its lead.

"Economic sanctions are unlikely to work."

As unpopular or uncomfortable as it may be, especially after two major hostage traumas and the rapidly increasing toll of American lives, the United States must then begin looking at the possibility of rapprochement with Iran. It is a bitter pill to swallow, but no other option is effective or practical for a democracy. Equally important, the war is unwinnable.

Realism Needed

Just a year ago, I would never have believed I would write these words, after watching rescuers dig through rubble at two American embassies and the Marine compound in Beirut looking for my friends, who were often recovered in bits and pieces. But a certain degree of realism is needed to avoid the loss of more lives, without America's seeming to cave in or concede.

The Iranian revolution is not a mirage, and the elimination of certain radical mullahs or activists will not make it or the militants' campaign disappear. Most Middle East experts agree that, despite Iran's many problems, Khomeinism—or Iran's Shiite form of rule based on Islam—is certain to survive Ayatollah Khomeini.

The United States needs to demonstrate the maturity and confidence of a superpower. Indeed, the outcome of this confrontation with Muslim extremists may depend more on the political initiative by the United States than on the success of Iranian progaganda and the training of suicide commandos at Iranian bases.

Rapprochement will not be quick or easy, especially for a nation where elections are held every four years. It will not reach fruition during the Reagan administration. And it will probably not happen during the lifetime of Ayatollah Khomeini. But that does not mean that the United States should not position itself by laying the groundwork earlier, which also might help save American lives during the period in between. The alternative is continued conflict and possible further escalation and higher death tolls.

Hopeful Signs

And there are some hopeful signs. "No matter how virulent their rhetoric, the Iranian leaders finally have come to believe that the very survival of their revolution will be in jeopardy if they fail to cope with mounting domestic political and economic pressures by breaking down the walls of their international isolation," Prof. Ramazani says.

In fact, Iran is moving to end its isolation. This year economic ties with Europe have almost returned to pre-revolutionary levels. Japan and West Germany are among Iran's main trading partners. Behind-the-scene contacts have begun with western states as well as Islamic rivals, including the Saudi foreign minister, who visited Tehran in May.

Iranians have also occasionally allowed pragmatic considerations to overshadow attempts to export their revolution, including the decision not to close the strategic oil lanes to the West through the Strait of Hormuz, comparative restraint in responding to Iraq's aerial strikes on tankers ferrying oil from Iran, and the ongoing, if troubled, relationship with other Muslim states in OPEC. The Iranians also did not retaliate when the Saudis aided by U.S. AWAC aircraft, shot down one of their planes in mid-1984.

"The use of force would also endanger our allies."

The major pragmatic consideration for Iran and the Shiite extremists is that the war with the United States is unwinnable, even though they can wreak havoc and destabilize governments along the way.

During the rapprochement process, neither side need succumb or lose face. No one need apologize or acknowledge fault since neither side can alter the past, or bring back the dead.

The United States could relay quiet messages through intermediaries that it recognizes that the Islamic Republic of Iran has a wide base of support and that the United States has no intention of repeating the CIA-sponsored operation that restored power to the shah in the 1950s—which would be folly anyway. Such messages would go a long way toward easing the tension.

Sending a message to Iran would also deal with what is at the core of the conflict and what the militants want from the United States: They are seeking respect and independence on equal terms instead of being looked at as client states or as pawns in bipolar games. They feel the United States is a threat because the Americans have a record of intervention. They use terror since it is the only effective weapon that an emerging movement can use to challenge a superpower.

Rapprochement Precedents

Precedents for rapprochement do exist—with the Soviet Union in the 1930s, after thousands of American troops, along with forces from 15 other nations, failed to stamp out the Bolshevik movement after World War I; and with China in 1972, after 23 years of a cold war, broken by two "hot" wars with Asian communists.

The theocratic regime in Iran, which has consolidated its hold on power, is now more secure than during the era when Carter attempted to improve relations to help end the United States' first hostage crisis. Indeed some Iranian leaders have even hinted at a willingness to begin contacts with the West again. In a speech to the Iranian parliament, Foreign Minister Ali Akbar Vellayati said last year: "The world is determined on the diplomatic scene. If we are not present, it will be determined without us."

The stakes are too high, the alternative too deadly, for the option of rapprochement to be discarded simply because it means acknowledgment of Iran, a former client state turned hostile, as a major new dynamic force. The goal must be to channel the growing destructive energies behind the Islamic Republic and the many arms of the militants' campaign into a constructive form.

As Ibn Khaldun, a famous 14th century Muslim philosopher, wrote: "Man's distinguishing characteristic is the ability to think . . . and through thinking to cooperate." The Koran itself demands of the faithful: "And if they incline towards peace, incline yourself also towards it."

Robin Wright, former Beirut correspondent of The Sunday Times *of London, is the author of* Sacred Rage: The Crusade of Militant Islam.

viewpoint 108

The US Should Leave Terrorist States

Charles William Maynes

There are two schools of thought for handling the terrorism threat emanating from Lebanon, including the hijacking crisis. Both are wrong. Neither being conciliatory nor being tough will work. Being realistic about the nature of Lebanon may.

Being conciliatory toward terrorists runs the risk of encouraging similar outrages against innocent Americans in the future. Almost no one supports conciliation.

The United States has already been tough in Lebanon. It ordered the battleship New Jersey to fire into the hills of Lebanon in an effort to shore up the authority of the Christian-dominated central government. At the time, in response to concern about innocent victims, U.S. officials claimed knowingly that to fire the New Jersey's guns was "like tossing a Volkswagen on a tennis court."

Then in early June, 1985, the U.S. Navy quietly announced that it was undertaking an extensive program to improve the accuracy of its recommissioned World War II battleships. It turned out that because the United States was using powder dating from the Korean War, shells from the New Jersey—each heavy as a Volkswagen—tended not only to hit intended targets but Lebanese villages.

The US Is Perceived Enemy

The result was to drive the Muslim majority of the country to the conclusion that the United States was the enemy. In the crazed atmosphere of Lebanese politics, the car bombing of the U.S. Embassy and the Marine barracks followed.

The legacy of hatred lives on. One of the hostages released in Algiers expressed confusion on her return to the United States: Why did the hijackers have such a hostile attitude toward New Jersey, the state she was from?

Charles William Maynes, "Neither Conciliation nor Toughness Is the Answer," *Los Angeles Times,* June 30, 1985. Reprinted with the author's permission.

Nor was the firing of the New Jersey's guns the only misplaced effort to use force to solve a Lebanon problem that has no short-run solution. In May, 1985, American newspapers reported that the Reagan Administration had authorized the CIA to train counterterrorist units composed of foreigners, including Lebanese who could strike suspected terrorists before they could attack U.S. targets, and that one unit in Lebanon, acting without authority, planted a car bomb that killed more than 80 civilians instead of the Shia leader the team had hoped to assassinate.

The hijackers of TWA flight 847 also cite this attack as a justification for their action. In response, the CIA, in a carefully worded statement, now points out that a House Intelligence Committee review of the incident found no CIA complicity in the bombing. But, of course, there can be no complicity in a runaway mission. There could be some residual responsiblity.

Preemptive US Action

The whole episode reveals why Secretary of State George P. Shultz's calls for preemptive U.S. action against terrorism—even at the risk of killing innocent civilians—are so misguided. After the runaway mission involving the car bombing, the United States rejected just such a policy, but no one in the rest of the world can be sure that this is the case. From now on, whenever assassinations occur in the Middle East, as they will, some parties may point to statements like those of Shultz as proof that the United States was behind the violent deed.

A senior official of Amal, the more moderate branch of Lebanon's Shia community, made this point when he commented that his chief, Nabih Berri, had lots of enemies in Lebanon but that after some U.S. statements, if anything happened to him, "all the Shias in the world will say the Americans are behind that, and no Americans in the Arab world will be safe after that." Some believe that better intelligence can resolve some of these dilemmas. But experienced American diplomats repeatedly warned the Reagan Administration against many of the actions that turned out to have such disastrous consequences. Some sections of Israeli intelligence are reported to have had grave reservations about the Ariel Sharon-Menachem Begin plan to prop up a Christian minority government in Lebanon, but the Israeli Cabinet ignored such warnings and plunged into the morass.

This latest incident is certain to reopen the questions of whether the congressional investigations of CIA abuses in the past have gutted the American intelligence effort. The United States has made grave mistakes. It allowed the Shah of Iran to order the State Department and the CIA not to maintain contact with the Iranian opposition. And the United States has overestimated the intelligence achievements of Israel, which, like America, has suffered severe setbacks from terrorists in Lebanon.

Strengthening the CIA

The Reagan Administration has spared no effort to strengthen the CIA. But it will take years of effort to penetrate such groups as the Lebanese Shias, more moved by religious visions than by CIA promises of a Swiss bank account. Many Western intelligence agencies had penetrated the leadership structure of the PLO, whose departure from Beirut ironically deprived Western governments of needed information, at least temporarily. But few have reliable agents among the new social groups that have thrust their way to the surface in the Middle East.

"Neither being conciliatory nor being tough will work."

Some in the United States, these problems notwithstanding, want to resume a policy of toughness. Some have wanted to bomb Iran, presumably as the base of Shia fervor. Others have proposed that the United States arrange to have a disproportionate number of Lebanese Shias shot, presumably from among any of the "detainees" still held in Israel. As in the Carter Administration during the Iranian hostage crisis, these suggestions are advanced not because they will help resolve the crisis but because some officials are trying to protect the President's domestic base of support.

It is time to be honest about this crisis. Israel's holding of about 700 Lebanese Shias has been illegal, using these people as hostages. The United States has always believed that Israel was wrong to invade Lebanon, wrong to seize the hostages and wrong to transfer them to Israel.

Israel claims that the fate of the Shias has not been connected in any way to the fate of the American hostages and that it intended in any event to release them. So be it. Israel should have released these people without comment or conditions as part of the effort to extract itself completely from its disastrous involvement in Lebanon.

Refusing to Negotiate

The United States should have made no comment on Israel's action. (The fact that the United States now has no ambassador in Israel makes it even more difficult to manage this sensitive issue.) It should also have refused to talk to those holding the U.S. hostages. No hint must be given, now or in any future hostage situations, that the United States will pay any price for release. The Administration should indicate that the future U.S. attitude toward Lebanon as a whole cannot be cooperative if the American hostage situation is not immediately resolved.

At some point in such incidents, third parties offer to intervene. In this instance, it is Syria, willing to hold, in Damascus, the American hostages until the Israelis complete the release of their Lebanese prisoners. The TWA passengers will be safer in Syria than in Lebanon. So a move to Syria is desirable. Nevertheless, the United States should not be party to negotiations with Syria over arrangements for a swap with Israel. There are three reasons:

First, since Israel insists the two issues are not linked, the United States should not itself link them by negotiating with the Syrians.

Second, a standing government like that in Syria should not act as a policeman for people seized illegally. It should understand that its obligation is the immediate release of the Americans.

Illegitimate Means

Third, governments should not be encouraged to believe they can pursue legitimate national goals through illegitimate means. Such prominent Israelis as Abba Eban have been pointing out that Syria, ironically, has proven a country on which Israel has been able to rely to respect an agreement, provided its terms can be worked out. The quiet border on the Golan Heights proves that thesis to be true. Yet there are few leaders in the Middle East more ruthless than Hafez Assad, the Syrian president. The United States does not want to encourage the authorities in Damascus to conclude that seizing Americans is a convenient way of forcing Washington to put pressure on Israel to accept Syrian demands.

The United States should also draw some lessons for the immediate future regarding the U.S. presence in Lebanon. The country is like a sick patient who has received whatever help modern medicine can provide but who remains ill and a danger to others through contagion. In such cases a quarantine is imposed until the danger to others passes.

Unnecessary Danger

In the short run, it makes no sense for the United States to expose its citizens in Lebanon to unnecessary danger when conditions make it almost impossible for them to carry on their professional duties. The U.S. government should order all American officials home and urge those holding U.S. passports to leave Lebanon until security conditions improve. This step should be taken even if there is a sudden resolution of the current crisis; for even before the recent hijacking, eight U.S. citizens in Lebanon were kidnapped.

In the long run, once the fever has passed, there will again be a major U.S. role in Lebanon. For Lebanon is a country of traders and bankers who can only survive with commercial energies turned outward. Once the internal struggle for power is settled, the new authorities will have a vested interest in restoring normal relations with the United States.

"It makes no sense for the United States to expose its citizens. . . to unnecessary danger when conditions make it almost impossible for them to carry on their professional duties."

A wise captain does not sail his vessel directly into a tidal wave. He waits for a calmer sea.

Israel's misadventure in Lebanon has created a human tidal wave, raised even higher by subsequent U.S. mistakes. The wave must subside before there can again be a responsible outside role in Lebanon.

Charles William Maynes is the editor of Foreign Policy *magazine.*

"The civilized powers must be prepared to act directly against the terrorist states."

The US Should Punish Terrorist States

Paul Johnson

Terrorism is the cancer of the modern world. No state is immune to it. It is a dynamic organism which attacks the healthy flesh of the surrounding society. It has the essential hallmark of malignant cancer: unless treated, and drastically, its growth is inexorable, until it poisons and engulfs the society on which it feeds and drags it down to destruction.

Modern terrorism dates from 1968, when the PLO formally adopted terror and mass murder as its primary policy. Terrorism was thus able to draw on the immense financial resources of the Arab oil states, and on the military training programs of the Soviet Union and of its satellites, Cuba, South Yemen, Vietnam and North Korea. Over 1,000 PLO killers have been trained in the Soviet Union alone. Moreover, from 1970-1982, the PLO operated a quasi-occupation of Lebanon, and was thus able to enjoy, in practice, all the advantages of a sizeable modern army, and set up terrorist training camps of its own, used as facilities by the Red Brigades, the IRA and a score of other killer gangs throughout the world.

This *physical* growth of the terrorist cancer was accompanied by a progressive elevation in its *moral* status. Yasser Arafat ceased to be a mere gangster leader and became, in effect, a terrorist Statesman. He moved around the world with increasing diplomatic pomp, and was greeted, on a level of moral equality, by more and more world leaders. He and his organization finally achieved, at the United Nations, a position of privilege granted to no other body not a sovereign state. But perhaps his greatest moral triumph was to be received, and photographed being greeted, by the Pope—his Holiness and his Depravity together.

Inevitably, with the physical and moral growth of the terrorist international, came a growth of its

Paul Johnson, from an address at the Jonathan Institute's Conference on International Terrorism held in Washington, DC, June 25, 1985.

military capacity. From the ability to kill individuals grew the ability to kill scores, then hundreds, now thousands. Not merely the PLO but its junior allies began to handle munitions on a prodigious scale. It is now common for the IRA, for instance, to stage killings involving two or three tons of high explosives. International terrorists operating in a score of countries now have the power to shoot down aircraft, destroy armored vehicles and destroy heavily-protected security posts. There is the danger, frighteningly obvious to all of us, that terrorists will eventually possess nuclear weapons, but a more immediate risk is that they will secure—perhaps already have secured—devastating modern equipment now moving into the inventories of official armies: high-speed machine pistols firing 1200 rounds a minute and almost soundless; lightweight grenade-launchers and mortars, squirtless flame-throwers, short-range portable anti-tank, shoulder fired multi-rocket launchers and, most alarming of all, the new generation of guided missile-throwers which have long ranges, are highly accurate, and can be carried and fired by one man or woman.

At whom will these devastating new weapons be aimed? The question is pointless. They are aimed at the world, at civilized society everywhere. They will be used not merely to destroy security forces, but ordinary civilians, men, women, children. For, just as there seems to be no upper limit to the terrorist's arsenal, so there is no lowest depth beyond which the terrorist cannot sink in his moral declension. So ask not for whom the terrorist bell tolls: it tolls for thee, and thee, and thee—for decent innocent people everywhere.

The First Terrorist States

But in the growth of the terrorist cancer, a still more sinister aspect even than the expansion of its arsenals, is the arrival of the first terrorist states. If Soviet Russia and four of its satellites actively train and arm terrorist movements, we now have the phenomenon of two regimes—Iran and Libya—which constitute terrorist states in themselves. These states do not merely finance, arm and train foreign terrorists, providing them with bases and havens; they operate their own official machinery of international terrorism.

Both Iran and Libya now deploy, as part of their official armed forces and government machinery, assisted and provisioned by their embassies and diplomats, heavily armed, highly-trained and totally ruthless gangs of killers, who roam the world seeking out and destroying political or religious opponents— or mere critics—and in the process killing and maiming bystanders and destroying property throughout the civilized West. These states conduct such policies of government terrorism while still enjoying all the privileges of sovereign status and all the protection of international law—membership in the UN and its agencies, access to the IMF and World Bank, to the International Court and the Vienna and Hague Conventions.

Iran and Libya illustrate the extent to which the terrorist cancer has established its grip on the world's health, and our paralytic failure to treat the disease. Let me remind you that four years ago Iran committed a gigantic crime of state terrorism: it seized all the occupants of the embassy of the United States—the greatest power on earth—and held them hostage. That crime goes unrepented and unpunished. Yet Iran still operates privileged embassies throughout the world to service its killers. It is still a member of the UN, where it can defend its policies of mass murder. It is now destroying the world's shipping in the Gulf—maritime terrorism on a gigantic scale—or to give it the old name, piracy. Will that go unpunished too?

Professional Terrorists

Or again, two months ago, one or more professional state terrorists, living in and working from the Libyan Embassy in London, murdered a young British policewoman, in broad daylight and in front of hundreds of people. Under the protection of the Vienna Convention, on whose provision Colonel Qadafi insisted down to the last comma, the killer or killers were allowed to leave the country without search or investigation. Here was a murderous dictator who has sponsored terrorism all over the world, who operates his own terror-squads, organizes and finances others, who has caused, extended or prolonged no less than ten civil and interstate wars in Africa, who is responsible for the deaths of at least a million people, and who openly proclaims his contempt for international order, here he is able to take the maximum possible advantage of the conventions which govern behavior between law-abiding states.

Thus, with the emergence of the Terrorist State, the

cancer has spread to the point where it is multiplying its cells from within the framework of world order. The inmates are taking over the asylum; the doctors are helping to spread the bacillus. There is, then, no alternative to drastic treatment.

I have three propositions to put forward—the first on the *moral* level, the second on the *legal* level, the third on the *military* level. On the moral level, let us clear our minds of cant. By this I mean let us reject the ambivalence with which civilized people often approach the problem of terrorism. They condemn terrorism in general and on principle, but there is often one particular group of terrorists which arouses their sympathy, for historical, radical, ethnic or ideological reasons, and whom they are not prepared to describe as terrorists, but rather as freedom-fighters and guerrillas. One case is a small section of the Irish community in the United States and its sympathy for the IRA. The IRA is beyond question one of the most evil and destructive terrorist movements on earth. But it could not exist without the regular financial support it receives from some otherwise law-abiding and peaceful American-Irish.

Countering Ambivalence

So I would counter this ambivalence in the civilized world by a simple proposition: there is no such person as a "good" terrorist, anywhere, at any time, in any circumstances. In fighting terrorism, there cannot be qualifications. Terrorism must be fought with the same absolute rigor with which the civilized powers once fought piracy and the international slave-trade. There were no "good" pirates. There were no "good" slavers. There can be no "good" gunmen.

"Iran and Libya illustrate the extent to which the terrorist cancer has established its grip on the world's health, and our paralytic failure to treat the disease."

And let us note, at the same time, that the gunmen, the terrorists, do not, and by their nature cannot, achieve legitimate political aims. Under no circumstances can democratic societies be the beneficiaries of terrorism. The only gainers are anarchy on the one hand, and totalitarianism on the other, the twin Frankensteins which threaten to overwhelm the democratic West.

Let me give you two examples of what I mean. The modern age of terrorism began in 1968 with the PLO. Today, 16 years later, the PLO and the other terrorist movements it has succoured, have racked up an appalling total of lives extinguished and property destroyed. But how far has the PLO progressed towards achieving its political ends? It has made no progress at all—it has, in fact, regressed. The Palestinian state is further away than ever. The Israeli state is stronger and more firmly established than in 1968. The victims have been the Arab States which harbored the gunmen. Jordan saved itself in 1970 because it threw them out. Lebanon perished because it lacked the courage to do the same. That is always the pattern: if the only beneficiaries of terrorism are totalitarian regimes, the chief victims are weak-minded democracies which lack the perception and courage to treat terrorism as a mortal enemy.

States as Victims

Again, take the IRA. They have killed over a thousand people, most of them their own countrymen, since 1968. But the unitary Irish state is as far away as before, and they themselves constitute the chief obstacle to its realization. Meanwhile, what has happened to the Irish Republic, which has throughout observed that fatal ambivalence toward terrorism which I have described? Its economy is in ruins, the very fabric of its state is under threat, and—since the IRA finances itself through the drug-trade—Ireland now has the biggest drug problem in Western Europe. No harm of any consequence has been inflicted on Britain—it is Ireland and her people who are the victims of the men with guns.

"Terrorism must be fought with the same absolute rigor with which the civilized powers once fought piracy and the international slave-trade."

Now let us look briefly at the *legal* level. If there are no "good" terrorists, it follows that civilized states must act collectively against all of them. Of course, the UN is useless—terrorist states are among its honored members. NATO is inappropriate. I put no faith in the European Anti-Terrorist Convention, even if everyone could be persuaded to sign it. Indeed, I put no faith in any formal treaty arrangement—you end up with a Vienna Convention. But I have a lot of faith in practical, informal and flexible arrangements between the major civilized powers.

We have to grasp the fact that to hurt one terrorist movement is to hurt them all. So I would like to see a coordinated, well-financed, informal and secret effort by the major civilized powers to discover and exchange information about movements, routes, identities, weapons stocks, methods, plans, codes, safe houses and bases of all terrorists everywhere. And it follows that we must be prepared to devise

and carry through concerted operations. The hydra is less likely to survive if struck simultaneously in several places. All the legitimate powers must have their trained anti-terrorist units, and they must be accustomed to acting in concert.

A Coordinated Defense

For the terrorist, there can be no hiding places. The terrorist must never be allowed to feel safe anywhere in the world. He must be made to fear he is being followed not just by agents of the government against which is is conspiring, but the agents of many governments, coordinated by a common system. A terrorist kept constantly on the defensive is an ineffective terrorist.

No hiding places—and that means, sooner or later, that the civilized powers must be prepared to act directly against the terrorist states. Looking back over the last two decades, we can claim some notable successes against individual terrorist movements. But these have been essentially defensive successes. Only on one occasion has a major offensive blow been dealt against the system of international terrorism itself. That was in 1982, when Israel crossed into Lebanon and expelled the PLO by force. The truth is, by having the moral and physical courage to violate a so-called sovereign frontier, and by placing the moral law above the formalities of state rights, Israel was able for the first time to strike at the heart of the cancer, to arrest its growth, and to send it into headlong retreat. That is the kind of thing I mean by drastic treatment.

I believe we should study the example set by the Israelis in 1982, and debate in what circumstances, and by what means, the civilized West as a whole will be prepared to act physically against the terrorist states in the future. I think it must be made clear to the master-killers of Teheran and Tripoli that there can be no ultimate hiding place for them either, that the arm of civilization is long and sinewy, and may be stretched out to take them by the throat. Let us in the West consider these possibilities. Let us have no formal treaties or arrangements. But let us debate privately among ourselves when, and if so how, we will be prepared to discard the obstacle of sovereignty and national frontiers, behind which the state killers shelter. Let us calmly and discreetly amass and train the forces which will be necessary for such police-action, and discuss how we will deal with the political and international consequences. Let us decide in good time the limits beyond which terrorist states will not be allowed to pass, and let us perfect a military instrument of fearful retribution when and if those limits ever are crossed.

I believe the knowledge that the civilized world has the courage and means to act in this manner will itself serve as a deterrent to state terrorism. I stress the word courage, and the physical preparedness without which courage is useless. For the cancer of terrorism feeds on weakness in all its forms—on all the hesitations and divisions and ambiguities inseparable from free, liberal societies. We must put these weaknesses behind us, and act, in Lincoln's words, with malice towards none—except the killers; with charity for all—especially their innocent victims; above all, with firmness in the right, as God gives us to see the right. We must, as the Book of Joshua puts it, ''Be strong and of good courage,'' for it is the combination of strength and courage which alone can arrest and destroy the terrorist cancer.

Paul Johnson is the author of Modern Times: The World from the Twenties to the Eighties.

The Ethiopian Famine: An Overview

Russ Watson, et al.

When a Red Cross relief station opened...in Bati, a remote township in northern Ethiopia, the local population quickly swelled from 3,000 people to 15,000—all of them hungry. "Today it's 25,000, and they're still coming," George Reid of the Red Cross said....Only the relatively fit make it to Bati. "One woman I met left home with her four children after her husband died," Getachew Araya, general secretary of the Ethiopian Red Cross reported after visiting Bati. "Three of them died on the road. The day after she arrived, the last child died. This is normal in Bati....I drove south from Bati to Addis. Starving children were lying on the road to stop food trucks. It took me five hours to travel 28 miles."

At times this year, it almost seemed that the entire population of Mozambique was on the move—all 14 million of them, searching for food. From countless "dead villages," dusty columns of lame, gaunt Africans trudged through the bush, some of them already blinded by malnutrition and clinging to their neighbors. "We have been hungry for three years," said a peasant woman named Elisa Ferro. "I have forgotten what it feels like to have a full belly."

In Mauritania, the earth and the sky meld into a uniform gray. In barely 20 years, the West African country has lost more than three-quarters of its grazing land to the encroaching sands of the Sahara. Rainfall has become another forgotten luxury. Last year's precipitation was the lowest in 70 years, and most of the grain crop failed. In some areas, 90 percent of the livestock died off. Now it is the people who are going hungry.

The Worst Famine

It is the worst famine in African history. Two vast belts of drought have spread across the continent,

parching the land and starving its inhabitants. Nearly 30 countries are officially listed as hungry, and in some of them, whole populations are in danger of extinction. Already, as many as 200,000 people may have died in Mozambique. In Ethiopia, the famine has helped kill at least 300,000 people, and an additional million may perish before the disaster is over. But the numbers are little more than guesswork. The precise dimensions of the tragedy remain unknown, merely suggested by the horror stories that trickle out of the back country or by the haggard hordes that appear almost nightly on Western TV. "What we know," the acting secretary-general of the Organization of African Unity, Peter Onu, said last week, "is that millions of our people are starving and hundreds of thousands are dying because we are no longer able to provide our own staple food."

Too Late for Many

There is something hideously wrong about people dying of famine when others have more food than they know what to do with. Tony Hall, an Ohio congressman, returned from a visit to Ethiopia last week complaining about precisely that inequity. "It is unconscionable," he said at a press conference, "that people on the other side of the globe should die of starvation while mountains of food—yes, literally mountains of food—pile up in our silos and warehouses." Last week the mountain was finally moving. In a vast outpouring of concern and generosity, relief agencies were deluged with contributions. Ethiopia, the country whose plight has received the most publicity so far, was swamped with more food than it could handle efficiently. But many Ethiopians were too far gone to be saved. "It was too late for many six months ago," a British relief worker said recently. "It is too late for others today and too late for many tomorrow."

The last big African famine occurred only 10 years

ago—leading, among other things, to the overthrow of Ethiopia's Emperor Haile Selassie and the creation of a Marxist state. About 300,000 Africans died in that famine, and at the time, some relief workers vowed that it would never happen again. The experts insist that famine is predictable, manageable and even preventable. But not this time. The first warnings of impending disaster, issued two years ago, were largely ignored by Western governments, relief agencies and news media—and by the Ethiopian regime itself. It was only last month that a British Broadcasting Corp. film alerted the world to a tragedy that, by then, was well under way in Ethiopia and other black African countries.

> *"Drought is, of course, a normal occurrence in Africa. But the effects are steadily getting worse because of Africa's deepening poverty, booming population and abuse of the land itself."*

Drought is, of course, a normal occurrence in Africa. But the effects are steadily getting worse because of Africa's deepening poverty, booming population and abuse of the land itself. Some Africans agree that part of the damage is self-inflicted—that mismanagement, corruption and civil strife aggravate the natural disasters that have always beset their societies. It is no coincidence that some of the nations suffering most from the current famine—Ethiopia, Mozambique, Chad, Angola—have been embroiled in civil war for years. None of that will change quickly. Nor will the famine go away overnight; with the best of weather, the hunger is likely to last until this time next year. "Even after the harvest then, substantial numbers of people will still need food," says Klaus Wiersing of the United Nations Disaster Relief Organization (UNDRO). "It won't be enough to feed people now and then forget about them."

Cruel Dilemmas

The rains finally came to Kenya in October, and last week parts of Mozambique were soaked by a downpour. The hunger remained. In Mozambique, village children were catching and eating tiny sparrows. Even the birds were emaciated, and they were becoming fewer in number. Kenya, a more prosperous country, has been able to limit human deaths. But hundreds of thousands of cattle, sheep, and goats have died, reducing the country's food potential for the next few years. Even with rain, Kenya must continue to rely on imported grain.

Cruel dilemmas come up all over central and southern Africa these days. Zimbabwe, where crop and cattle losses are heavy, has been swamped by 50,000 refugees from neighboring Mozambique. Now the government has ordered its border patrols to turn back starving Mozambicans, "ruthlessly if necessary." "They treat us as though the drought is all our fault," complains one of the refugees, Maria Ntape. Dr. Simbi Mubako, Zimbabwe's minister of home affairs, maintains: "We cannot improve the living standards of our own citizens if foreigners keep adding to the numbers."

Living standards are declining everywhere. For three years, Jane Comstock, a Peace Corps desk officer, has been watching Niger deteriorate. "Now it's really astounding," she says, recalling a September visit. "There are people eating on three- and four-day cycles: the children eat once every three days, and the adults eat once every four days." Comstock also reports signs of a cholera epidemic in Niger, Mali, Burkina Faso (formerly Upper Volta) and Senegal.

In Ethiopia, relief supplies were beginning to show up in quantity, and dignitaries like U.N. Secretary-General Javier Perez de Cuellar arrived to show their concern. The first food trucks reached the northern town of Korem in a military convoy, for protection against rebels. "We had been here for eight months, screaming for food, and yet none was arriving," Dr. Michel Corvalet, a French physician who works at the Korem refugee camp, said by telephone from Addis Ababa. More than 50,000 people were waiting at the camp for food, and there wasn't enough to go around. Before the convoy came in, about 100 people were dying every day; afterward the average dropped to somewhere between 30 and 50. Doctors were forced to perform a gruesome act of triage, selecting only the hardiest refugees to receive food and clothing. The physicians would work their way through the teeming crowds, using marking pencils to place crosses on the foreheads of those who stood the best chance of survival. Aid could not be wasted on the weak.

The refugees squatted out of doors, exposed to the fierce daytime sun and the harsh cold air that settles over the mountainsides at night. The food station at Alamata attracted more than 5,000 members of the nomadic Afar tribe, who line up each day for a small ration of grain. They weren't allowed to stay inside the compound at night, for fear that they might admit rebel attackers. They weren't allowed to build huts outside the compound, for fear that they will settle down; the government wants them to go back to where they came from.

Forgetting How to Eat

Many refugees were so debilitated that they could not swallow or digest food when it finally became available to them. The answer was "wet-feeding"—mixing grain with water so that it will go down easier—but in many camps there was a shortage of clean water. Some small children had a slightly different problem: they had to be hand-fed because they had forgotten how to eat. Starvation brought other ailments with it, including influenza, measles, tuberculosis, diarrhea, smallpox, typhus and kwashiorkor, a protein deficiency that lightens the skin, reddens the hair and bloats the bellies of malnourished children. In most refugee camps, there was no medicine for such maladies. At Alamata, a group of mothers recently brought their children in for treatment of pneumonia. "I am sorry," said Dr. George Ngatire, a Kenyan. "There is nothing I can do. I know your children need treatment, but I have nothing to treat them with. Come back in five days."

Getting food to Ethiopia was a lot easier than actually delivering it to the people most in need. The main port at Assab and the airfield at Addis Ababba were badly jammed. Roads leading to the interior were clogged, and there was a shortage of vehicles and fuel. "Sometimes it is a question of too much at once without coordination," Hans Einhaus, the director of UNDRO, said in Geneva. "The response in the case of Ethiopia was magnificent, but now we have 54 aircraft waiting to be unloaded at an airport which normally can deal with just three or four planes a day. Everyone wants to be the first to send in relief, but that is not always a good thing. There are cases of wasted food, although it is difficult for us to say so because of the danger that people might stop giving."

Inappropriate Aid

Not all of the relief supplies were appropriate. The Soviet Union contributed 10,000 tons of rice, which Ethiopians didn't like. A British shipment turned out to include cases of whiskey, apparently intended for delegates to last week's OAU summit in Addis Ababa. Unsuitable relief supplies seem to be a feature of every major disaster; the West Germans, for some reason, always send field hospitals, whether they're especially needed or not.

"With everyone getting into the assistance act, there often are serious problems," says one relief official. "The various agencies within the U.N. itself compete against each other for image-building purposes, preferring to send their own individual shipments without any clear notion of how the food or other aid can ever get to the actual people in need." Sometimes the same criticism is made of private, voluntary agencies, which depend upon the contributions generated by a sympathetic public response to major disasters. "One agency in a certain recent case flew in 150 tons of food when 150,000 tons were required," says Einhaus. "If that had been put together with donations by others, the total could have been reached and distributed." But private organizations, like official agencies, sometimes don't care to submerge their own identities in a common cause.

In this case, the Ethiopian government was partly to blame for the severity of the disaster. The country's leader, Lt. Col. Mengistu Haile Mariam, was warned of impending famine in 1982, in a report from a group of experts headed by Keith Griffin, an Oxford University economist. The Griffin team recommended immediate food rationing and heavy new emphasis on rural development. Mengistu ignored the advice. Instead, he poured 46 percent of Ethiopia's gross national product into military spending, buying at least $2.5 billion worth of arms from the Soviet Union. What investment he did make in agriculture was concentrated on building Soviet-style state farms—hardly a promising model, in view of the fact that the Soviets can't even feed themselves. When the famine began, Mengistu's regime covered it up, apparently to keep from spoiling the $200 million party that was being thrown to celebrate the 10th anniversary of the revolution. Only when the celebration was over did the government allow foreign journalists to visit areas that, by then, were blighted by famine.

US Responded Slowly

The United States responded slowly at first to the looming crisis. At the World Bank meeting last September, France proposed a special-aid program for Africa. "The Americans weren't interested, to say the least," recalls Dominique Brustel, an official of the French Ministry for Cooperation. "They blocked the funds." Critics of the Reagan administration charge that Ethiopia's status as a Soviet ally inhibited U.S. relief. "The hungry kids are seen by some downtown as 'little commies,' so the grain just sits there," charges one agricultural expert on Capitol Hill, Democratic Sen. Patrick Leahy of Vermont.

"Many refugees were so debilitated that they could not swallow or digest food when it finally became available to them."

So far, the administration has refused to tap a reserve grain stock that was created last year for emergencies like the African famine. But it has donated grain from other sources. Just last week, the U.S. Agency for International Development (AID) earmarked 137,000 tons of grain, worth $57.5 million, for Ethiopia, Mozambique, Mauritania and Chad. In terms of tonnage, U.S. food aid in the current fiscal year, which began only on Oct. 1, already exceeds the amount donated during the entire previous year. The political overtones, however, are loud and clear. "The word is out that the West delivers the food," boasts AID administrator M. Peter

McPherson, who recently returned from Ethiopia. Other American officials still hope that U.S. relief may represent ''a threat to Soviet hegemony over Ethiopia,'' as one of them puts it.

Africa's dependence on relief aid will probably grow in the years ahead. A study issued last week by the Swedish Red Cross and by Earthscan, a London-based environmental news service, reports that ''events called 'natural disasters' are killing more and more people every year. Yet there is no evidence that the climatological mechanisms associated with droughts, floods and cyclones are changing.'' Instead, the report says that the effects of natural disasters are worsened by poverty, environmental damage and rapid population growth.

Food Supply Inadequate

Black Africa is the world's poorest area, and it is the only region in which the population is growing faster than the food supply. Agriculture never fully recovered from the devastating drought of a decade ago. In 1982, Ethiopia's per capita food production was only 81 percent of what it was in 1969-1971; in Mozambique, the figure was 68 percent. On average, African governments spend four times as much on armaments as they do on agriculture. Primitive farming, in turn, has devastated the environment.

''The United States responded slowly at first to the looming crisis.''

Under increasing pressure for production, traditional fallow periods have been shortened, wearing out the soil. Most farmers have no chemical fertilizers, and the animal dung that they once used to enrich the soil is now being burned for fuel. That's because so many trees have been cut down. Only 20 years ago, 16 percent of Ethiopia's land area was covered by forest; today the figure is just 3.1 percent. ''With deforestation, the soil loses much of its capacity to retain moisture and consequently its productivity and resistance to drought,'' says U.N. environmentalist Seifulaziz L. Milas.

There is reason to believe that relief shipments, though necessary, only aggravate the fundamental problems. ''Food aid saves lives but can also undermine long-term local self-sufficiency,'' says the Earthscan report. The study concludes that ''disaster assistance must go hand in hand with development assistance.'' There is much that could be done. Many African nations ought to raise their artificially low food prices, in order to encourage farmers. Large areas need reforestation, perhaps with fast-growing species such as the eucalyptus tree. Many countries should strike a better balance between food crops and cash crops raised for export; Chad recently reaped a bumper cotton harvest, but its people are dying for want of homegrown food.

Above all, governments must spend money on agricultural development. ''I believe Africa can become a granary for a large part of the world, but there has not been a very major investment until now,'' William Clark, president of the International Institute for Environment and Development, said recently. Time is running out. Without the right investment of effort and money, Black Africa is more likely to become a charnel house than a granary.

Russ Watson is a reporter for Newsweek, *a weekly national news magazine.*

"The starvation in Ethiopia is man-made....The destruction of Ethiopian agriculture was...not a natural calamity, but the result of ideologically dictated government policy."

viewpoint **111**

Communism Caused the Ethiopian Famine

Robert W. Lee

Ethiopia is Africa's oldest independent country. Sadly, it has within the past decade been transformed into one of that continent's most doctrinaire and unyielding Communist dictatorships. As a result, a culture which dates back to Old Testament times, and a land which once served as an African breadbasket, have been laid waste by famine and cruelty.

Since seizing power in 1977, the Marxist regime of Lieutenant Colonel Mengistu Haile Mariam abandoned traditional agricultural practices, disrupting food production without providing a viable alternative. As summarized by the Heritage Foundation: "Traditionally, Ethiopian peasants have saved food in good years to prepare for bad harvests. The government outlawed this practice, branding it as hoarding. Peasants traditionally invested money earned from surplus crops in their own farms to expand production. This was denounced as capitalist accumulation. Independent food traders traditionally bought food in food-surplus areas and transported it to markets in food-deficient areas. This was outlawed as exploitation, and government commissions replaced the free market."

Britain's *Economist* recently recalled that, following the overthrow of Haile Selassie in 1974, "church and crown lands, which amounted to half the total arable land, were dished out haphazardly to the peasants, most of whom got plots of no more than a few hectares. The few well-run coffee and cotton estates were broken up. Huge state-owned farms were established," to which the Mengistu Government gave "more than their share of seed, fertilizer, credit and capital investment." The result was predictable: "...plenty of large tractors and machinery, but few projects of the sort the peasants need most: small dams, grain storage pits and silos, simple irrigation channels."

In 1982 a team of agricultural experts led by Oxford University economist Keith Griffin warned of impending famine and recommended measures to blunt its impact. The Mengistu regime ignored the advice, opting instead to continue the expenditure of nearly half (forty-six percent) of the nation's Gross National Product on military weapons, accompanied by further collectivization of the farms.

Starvation Is Man-Made

Syndicated columnist Jeffrey Hart is correct in asserting: "It is gradually beginning to seep into public consciousness that the starvation in Ethiopia is man-made....The destruction of Ethiopian agriculture was...not a natural calamity, but the result of ideologically dictated government policy. Once again, Marxism is doing what it does most efficiently, producing hunger and refugees."

Rather than allow Mengistu's Marxist experiment to collapse of its own brutality and false doctrine, economic assistance from the West in general, and the United States in particular, has propped up this cruel dictatorship. Between 1978 and 1982, Ethiopia received one billion dollars in aid from the West, most of it channelled through the various multilateral lending agencies (such as the International Monetary Fund) to which the United States contributes heavily. The Heritage Foundation observes: "This aid helped Mengistu suppress private enterprise and supplant it with state monopolies." And Philip Jacobson, writing in *The Times* of London for November 10, 1984, adds that much of the aid has been "routinely diverted into projects designed to bolster Colonel Mengistu's regime."

For its part, the U.S. Government directly supplied Ethiopia with some 41,488 metric tons of food valued at $22.7 million during Fiscal 1984, before the famine was documented on film and had to be admitted by

"Famine in Ethiopia" by Robert W. Lee first appeared in the April, 1985 issue of *American Opinion* (Belmont, Massachusetts 02178) and excepts are reprinted by permission of the publisher.

Mengistu. So far in the current Fiscal Year, our government has obligated more than $127 million in humanitarian assistance involving almost 223,000 metric tons of food, transportation costs, and medical supplies. Where most of it goes, nobody knows, since much of it is sent to the government-controlled Ethiopian Relief and Rehabilitation Commission. A State Department briefing paper released in January 1985 further informs us: "On November 2, 1984, the U.S. and Ethiopia agreed to a government-to-government humanitarian assistance program under which the U.S. is providing 50,000 metric tons of food *directly to the Ethiopian Government."* (Emphasis added.)

"The Mengistu regime has steadfastly refused to participate in a food truce with the rebels, and is instead purposely *aggravating the famine conditions."*

Does anyone believe that the Communist regime will use windfalls of that sort to feed starving Ethiopians rather than feather (and fortify) its own corrupt nest?

Once the food shipments reach the Ethiopian Relief and Rehabilitation Commission, or the government itself, accountability ends. Reports of abuse are legion, including food supplies which have completely disappeared, others which have been used in lieu of cash to pay laborers; the sale of relief food to peasants by soldiers who presumably pocket the receipts; the use of grain to pay the so-called "People's Militia" in Eritrea, subsidizing a Communist war of conquest with relief aid siphoned from humanitarian shipments; the use of food to feed military personnel and to help reimburse the Soviet Union for weapons purchases; the sale of food to Sudan and Egypt to provide cash for Mengistu's regime; *etc., etc.*

It was on October twenty-third and twenty-fourth of last year that a five-minute British Broadcasting Corporation report rebroadcast in the United States by NBC brought to public attention the extent of the Ethiopian tragedy and sparked the massive outpouring of humanitarian aid to those suffering from the famine. Only then did the crisis which had been developing for more than a year suddenly become a major news event. Here, according to the reliable and informative *AIM Report* in January 1985, is how it all came about:

Journalists Denied Visas

After pressing many months for visas to enter Ethiopia, Kenyan cameraman Mohammed Amin and BBC correspondent Michael Buerk "were finally admitted on October 16, 1984. They were given an

itinerary by the Ethiopian Relief and Rehabilitation Commission which did not include visits to any of the refugee camps. Amin had decided against doing the trip on that basis, but when he went back to the commission he found an 'acting official' in charge. The official tried to get in touch with those responsible for handling the press, but they were all out of the country. He decided to let Amin and Buerk visit the camps." Thus did the two journalists gain access to the Makalle and Korem camps to shoot the five-minute videotape which horrified the Western world and generated the massive outpouring of international (primarily U.S.) assistance.

Without in any way questioning the motives of reporters Amin or Buerk, some observers have wondered if that apparent blunder by the nameless "acting official" might not, in fact, have been set-up. Has the "acting official" been disciplined for violating *well-established policy* in a way that appears at first glance to be highly damaging to the Mengistu regime? Or has he been rewarded for "blundering" in a way that has brought a virtual cornucopia of foreign assistance which has served to strengthen the Communist Government at the further expense of the starving masses?

Before dismissing such a conclusion as bizarre, consider for a moment: What could be more consistent with the long record of Communist manipulation of food supplies and famines on the one hand, and the humanitarian instincts of non-Communists on the other? . . .

Government Aggravates Famine

Sixty to eighty percent of the Ethiopians who are now being starved by this Communist regime reside in rural areas controlled by the Eritrean and Tigrean rebel forces referred to earlier. The Mengistu Government does not allow relief operations in those areas and relief agencies are reluctant to attempt to circumvent the Government's policy for fear of losing their access to other areas of the country as well. The Mengistu regime has steadfastly refused to participate in a food truce with the rebels, and is instead *purposely* aggravating the famine conditions in the obvious hope of bringing the rebels to their knees as the Army has been unable to do. It has, for example, attacked food convoys on their way to famine victims in areas that the regime is trying to starve into submission. And, earlier this year, it seized from an Australian relief ship some six thousand tons of food (worth $1.2 million) intended for transshipment to Eritrea and Tigre. The confiscation was justified, the Communist Government claimed, because the Australian offer of food collected by volunteer agencies constituted "an infringement of Ethiopia's sovereignty" and was "tantamount to interference in our internal affairs."

Senator Al D'Amato (R.-New York) considers what is happening in northern Ethiopia to be reminiscent of the "horrible memories of what Josef Stalin's Soviet regime did to millions in the Ukraine. It's a pattern that has been repeated all too often, as we have seen recently in Afghanistan and Cambodia. The basic premise is simple: if you can't have total control over the people, kill them—by starvation if necessary."

Massive Relocation Program

Using the famine as an excuse, the Red hierarchy has also launched a massive relocation program which seeks to move as many as 1.5 million people from the northern provinces to the south. It is claimed that the move will better the lot of those involved, but it is in fact simply another politically motivated ploy aimed at getting as many peasants as possible out of the way in Eritrea and Tigre to make it that much easier to identify and capture (or kill) the rebel element. There has been little preparation in the south to care for, or even feed, the refugees. It is for this reason, among others, that anti-Communists in Tigre are convinced that Mengistu actually intends to wipe them out rather than simply move them to more fertile territory. As the *Wall Street Journal* editorialized on February 20, 1985, "it would not be the first time genocide has been disguised as resettlement." As, for instance, in Cambodia.

The resettlement scheme has meanwhile absorbed thousands of helicopter and truck hours which could have been devoted to the transport of food instead of people. And, though claimed to be voluntary, the program has been plagued with defectors seeking to return to their homelands. Refugees who escaped The Sudan from the Asosa resettlement camp have testified that Ethiopian soldiers, in a single month, killed 330 persons who attempted to escape.

The Mengistu regime has consistently accorded famine relief a low priority. Rather than being used to enhance the distribution of food, for instance, Army vehicles have instead been assigned to patrol roads to keep starving peasants from entering cities. Ethiopian authorities refused for some time to grant preferential treatment to food shipments from the West in congested Ethiopian ports. According to the *New York Times* for September 20, 1984, even Soviet cargo ships transporting cement were given priority over Western ships carrying food. And, when the food supplies were at last unloaded, an import tax of $12.50 per ton and a handling/trucking charge of $165 per ton were imposed. Even then, tons of food were left to rot while awaiting inland transportation.

Aid and the Soviet Union

The Communist Mengistu regime has also worked tirelessly to convey the impression that the food aid which is pouring into the country largely orginates in the Soviet Union. That has been achieved by having the Soviets deliver food after it arrives from the West, and by showing on Ethiopian televison only Soviet

planes said to be arriving with food. (Soviet food contributions have not only been meager, but outrageously inappropriate. For example, the Soviets supplied rice (Ethiopians are not rice eaters) and a shipment of salt (a commodity which Ethiopia exports).)

Many Western observers have speculated that the Mengistu regime camouflaged the extent of the famine for as long as it did to avoid tarnishing the September 1984 festivities (which cost from $150 million to $200 million) celebrating the tenth anniversary of the 1974 revolution. At the same time, an Ethiopian Communist Party (formally titled the Ethiopian Workers' Party) was launched, with delegations from more than fifty Red nations in attendance to hear Mengistu officially declare the country to be "Marxist-Leninist."

Imported Luxuries

The festivities included $500,000 worth of whiskey imported for the occasion, an expenditure which was widely publicized in Britain (where it stirred a good deal of anger), but received minimal attention in the United States where NBC reported it in one sentence while ABC and CBS ignored it entirely. And, as noted in January by *AIM Report:* "The celebrants were able to enjoy a new statue of V.I. Lenin, which reportedly cost $5 million. They were able to enjoy color television, another luxury which the government introduced at a cost of millions of dollars." Meanwhile, officials of the Catholic Relief Service estimated that at least two hundred and fifty persons per day starved to death in the northern provinces during the celebration.

"The Mengistu regime has consistently accorded famine relief a low priority."

And, lest we forget, the humanitarians at the United Nations are also concerned about the situation in Ethiopia. On October 16, 1984, the General Assembly's Fifth (Administrative and Budgetary) Committee voted eighty-three to three (the minority consisted of the U.S., Britain, and The Netherlands) to allocate $73.5 million in U.N. funds to the beleaguered country. But rather than helping the hungry, the money was specifically earmarked to improve conference facilities of the U.N.'s Economic Commission for Africa in Addis Ababa. In the wake of widespread criticism for this wildly inappropriate priority, a U.N. spokesman firmly maintained that the upgraded facilities were "sorely" needed because "the support facilities at Africa Hall are wholly inadequate for the needs of the ECA." The appropriation was subsequently ratified (122 to 5) by the General Assembly, at which time U.S.

Representative to the U.N. Richard Nygard noted that the $73.5 million could have inoculated one million Ethiopian children, built 25,000 wells and pumps for 12.5 million people, fed 125,000 Ethiopian families for a year with enough left over to supply all 1985 cereal imports for drought-stricken Chad. The U.S. share of the ECA facilities boondoggle is twenty-five percent, or about $18.4 million. All told, U.S., Western European, and Japanese funds will cover sixty percent (around $45 million) of the bill for the new conference center. As for the famine-stricken masses, let them eat plaster!

Stop Financing Communism

The western assistance sent to Ethiopia to date has benefitted the cruel Marxist Government far more than it has the starving masses for which it was intended. Considering the nature of Communism, we would hardly expect otherwise. It is a frustrating dilemma which underscores once again that the most humanitarian contribution the United States could make to alleviate the suffering in Ethiopia and other Communist-occupied countries would be to adopt and implement a foreign policy aimed at firmly assisting peoples oppressed by Marxist-Leninist dictatorships to throw off their chains. And the most important single plank in such a foreign policy would be to compel our own government to *stop financing Communism* through aid, trade, and every other means.

Robert W. Lee is a graduate of the University of Utah. He is a contributing editor for The Review of the News, *author of* The United Nations Conspiracy, *and is co-author of* A Taxpayer Survey of the Grace Commission Report.

"The starvation that we now see is the result of the difference between a growth in population of 3 percent per year and in food output of 2 percent."

Population Growth Caused the Ethiopian Famine

Lester Brown

Question: Mr. Brown, why does the tragedy of famine continue to be so massive and chronic throughout Africa?

Answer: Three forces are acting in concert to put African on the skids in terms of food supplies.

First, Africa now is experiencing the fastest population growth of any continent at any time in human history.

Second, the continent is undergoing widespread soil erosion from Mediterranean countries in the north all the way to the Cape of Good Hope in the south.

Third, African governments have neglected agriculture, giving it low priority in public investment and following food-price policies that placate urban consumers, thus discouraging farmers.

All three of these forces are now converging in a truly devastating fashion. What we are seeing is a situation that's been in the making for many years but has only now been brought into sharp focus by a severe drought.

Question: How much longer will the situation deteriorate?

Answer: Actually there is nothing to arrest the decline. That's the tragedy. That is the problem that is being missed in news coverage of the current situation in Africa.

Population and Starvation

Question: What do you mean?

Answer: In Africa as a whole, per capita grain production peaked around 1967 and has been sliding downhill ever since. There is every reason to believe that the slide will continue. The reason I say this is quite simple: Growth of African grain production has slacked off to a feeble rate of only 2 percent a year. At the same time, population—the number of mouths to feed—is growing by some 3 percent.

In simple terms, the starvation that we now see is the result of the difference between a growth in population of 3 percent per year and in food output of 2 percent.

There's no sign of change in either of these trends. The arithmetic at this point is pretty grim.

Question: Of the three problems, which is the most serious and should get greatest attention?

Answer: Population growth. What you have to keep in mind is that a population growing at 3 percent per year multiplies twentyfold in a century. Some African countries are a third of a century into that growth curve. Population growth is going to be checked, either because birth rates decline or because death rates rise.

Question: Why do you say this is the most serious problem?

Answer: It appears that population growth is causing climate change in Africa by its effect on land use. Changes in land use associated with population growth—conversion of forest to cropland, grassland to desert—increase water runoff and reduce the amount that evaporates into the clouds to return ultimately as rain.

Today, much of the rain runs off directly to the ocean and relatively little comes back up to recharge clouds. This is a double problem. There is not only a diminishing supply of water for crops, but the dry soil also turns into dust and blows away. It is becoming a vicious circle.

People and Resources

Question: What this cycle of deterioration of land use evident in the decades of colonial rule in Africa?

Answer: Historically, Africa had a relative balance between people and resources. However, this was achieved in harsh ways—largely because diseases kept population growth in check. With medical and sanitation advances of recent decades, in the absence of family planning, there has been an enormous increase in population pressure on land.

It's a major new threat that's beginning to surface. We may be on the edge of an unfolding human drama like nothing we've ever experienced before.

Question: Rather than chalking up the famine to natural forces—drought, pestilence, that sort of thing—you seem to be saying that there is also a human element.

Answer: As a matter of fact, what I'm saying is that this crisis is largely due to the human element because it's population growth that's causing changes in land use. Changes in land use are altering the water cycle. As that goes on, you would expect the amount of moisture that moves inland to be reduced. That is precisely what is happening. So, turning the situation around is going to take an enormous effort.

Question: How large an effort do you believe is needed?

Answer: We're not talking about something like a 30 percent increase in World Bank loans, that sort of thing. What I mean is massive reforestation, soil conservation, water development and conservation, family planning on a continental scale and with an urgency that we just have not seen before. It would compare with mobilization of the Western Allies for World War II in the early 1940s.

Reforestation Success

Question: Can even such a massive mobilization make a dent in problems of such huge dimensions?

Answer: We can look around the world and see at least a few countries that have been successful. South Korea is a model of reforestation; Israel has demonstrated clearly that the deserts can be reclaimed. Kenya has developed a fairly successful soil-conservation program. In agriculture, China has demonstrated very dramatically the value of letting market forces operate in response to price incentives.

Question: But won't it take decades to reverse the deterioration?

Answer: No. It could be years rather than decades. Certainly, it would be possible to see a difference by the end of the 1980s. We know the kinds of things that need to be done. It's a matter of getting things organized. Somewhere along the way, someone has to take the lead in this effort.

Question: Is there evidence that Western countries are ready for a long-term effort of such scope and magnitude?

Answer: Not much, not yet. The European countries possess a better understanding of what's happening in Africa and the need to help. And working with the World Bank, there is a very substantial commitment of resources, the better part of a billion dollars over the next several years.

That's important. But what needs to be done in Africa is not the sort of thing that the World Bank is experienced in doing. It's not a case of starting a few billion-dollar projects here and there or that sort of thing. What's needed is millions of people planting trees and building terraces on cropland and doing that kind of thing. It has to be a very labor-intensive process. Governments of Africa simply must be centrally involved and committed....

Question: How many African governments are now ready to move?

Answer: Many of the governments do not yet understand what's happening to them. I think there's still a feeling that the problem is drought, that droughts by definition come to an end. And then when the drought comes to an end, things will go back to normal and everything will be all right.

If that's correct, then muddling through as in the past will work. If it's not correct, then what's happening could become very costly. There's no guarantee the governments of Africa will understand soon enough and act in response.

Prerequisites for Aid

Question: Should the U.S. make drastic economic and agricultural reform a prerequisite for expanding its aid?

Answer: I think so. If we are to assume a burden for helping African nations, then we have an obligation not just to provide food aid as they need it but to try to attack the sources of the problems. Responding to a patient's need by treating only the symptoms often aggravates the illness.

The U.S. historically has done this. One of the reasons that India today is self-sufficient in food is because the U.S. government, using its food aid as a lever back in the late '60s, pressured the Indians to introduce essential and long-overdue agricultural policy reforms. So there's a precedent and an obligation for doing this sort of thing.

"What's happening may not be limited to Africa; I think these sorts of tests will come up in other places and manifest themselves in other ways."

Question: Given the fact that Ethiopia, the worst victim of famine, is ruled by a Marxist regime, isn't there likely to be strong resistance to such pressure from the U.S.? Wouldn't it be better to channel American aid through international organizations to avoid these political difficulties?

Answer: My judgment is that chances for major reforms in Ethiopia are much better if a strong multilateral agency like the World Bank is the donor or if the U.S. government provides food aid directly—with strings attached—rather than through a multilateral agency.

Certainly, looking back at reforms in India in the late '60s, President Johnson's decision to adopt a "short tether" food policy was instrumental in bringing about reforms in Indian agriculture, reforms that the Agriculture Minister knew were long overdue but which the Finance Minister didn't want to support.

If that aid had simply been handed to the Indians, then five or 10 years later India would have faced another crisis of even more serious proportions. Instead, it was given to them month by month, on condition that they do the things that they knew they had to do. This should also be done with Ethiopia, painful as it may be.

Accepting Change

Question: Do you think that the leaders in Addis Ababa would be willing to accept those conditions?

Answer: I don't know. They would probably get their backs up. But the Ethiopian record is becoming quite obvious. The evidence of failure could not be more dramatic. We should force them to re-examine their policies. Now, it is obviously possible to misuse food aid when the political purposes of governments get involved. But it seems to me that the mere provision of food aid itself is a political act. And if American food aid simply permits mismanagement to continue, then ask yourself whether that's appropriate.

Question: If Ethiopia balks and accepts the risk of even greater starvation, can the U.S. realistically allow that to happen?

"It is obviously possible to misuse food aid when the political purposes of governments get involved. But it seems to me that the mere provision of food aid itself is a political act."

Answer: No, we should stop short of that. The question that must be put to the governments in Africa, including the one in Ethiopia, is this: Are you prepared to assume the responsibility for feeding your people? If so, there are certain economic requirements for doing that. And we should be monitoring their progress and relentlessly pressing them to adopt the necessary reforms. Otherwise the situation will worsen further.

Question: As a practical matter, should the U.S. concentrate its aid and advice to African nations that are willing to make such good-faith reforms?

Answer: Yes. But because population growth seems to be driving climate change, it's not a matter where the United States can say, "We like this country, and we like that country and these two countries up here, and we're going to help them." It's a continental problem.

What we're seeing in Africa is the first instance where the deteriorating relationship between people and natural support systems is reaching the breakdown point. Africa is the first major test of whether the global community is capable of responding to this threat. What's happening may not be limited to Africa; I think these sorts of tests will come up in other places and manifest themselves in other ways.

Question: Your bottom line for Africa seems pretty pessimistic—

Answer: The situation in Africa is grim, and I don't think we've begun yet to understand that we're in the process of a long-term deterioration. It's not hopeless or irreversible. But the situation will not be reversed easily.

Lester Brown is president of Worldwatch Institute, a Washington-based research group. He was project director for the institute's report State of the World—1985.

"Those who invest in South Africa, invest in a system which we have described as being as evil, as un-Christian, as immoral as Communism ever was, as Nazism ever was."

Apartheid Remains an Inhumane System

Desmond Tutu

I first discovered that there were black people in the United States when I was a small boy of about eight years of age, and I picked up a battered copy of *Ebony* magazine. I didn't know that there could be literature of that kind, with such subversive qualities, because up to that point I had come to begin to believe what white people said about us. And, picking up *Ebony* magazine, I grew inches. I didn't know baseball from ping pong then—I don't think I do very much even now—but on that occasion I read about one Jackie Robinson breaking into major league baseball and that did wonders for me as a person.

Oppression the Ultimate Evil

Now, only those who have been victims of oppression and injustice and discrimination know what I am talking about when I say that the ultimate evil is not the suffering, excruciating as that may be, which is meted out to those who are God's children. The ultimate evil of oppression, and certainly of that policy of South Africa called apartheid, is when it succeeds in making a child of God begin to doubt that he or she is child of God. That is the ultimate blasphemy, and part of your mission has been helping us to recover the fact that we too have a share in this wonderful heritage which St. Paul calls the glorious liberty of the children of God.

And so, as young boys and girls in South Africa we were told on the one hand that you couldn't make it. But we knew on the other of the exploits of the Brown Bomber. I recall how we went through agonies. I don't know whether you remember when Joe Louis was fighting against Billy Conn. But I recall how we were biting our nails because it didn't seem like he was going to win that particular fight. It went on and on and on, and I don't want to tell you the

state of our stomachs as the fight progressed, and the yells of delight and the sighs of relief which we breathed out when the Brown Bomber did what he did so well on many another occasions and laid him straight.

I recall, too, seeing our first all-black film, *Stormy Weather*. I don't know whether it was a very good film. I don't know what the critics would say. But I don't care. Because for us it was making a political statement, it was making a theological statement. They were just putting together a piece of entertainment, a movie—Fats Waller, Cab Calloway, Lena Horne. Yet it was making a theological statement. It was saying that these whom you see depicted there have the *imago dei*. That these too are created in the image of God and if they are created in the image of God they too are God's representatives and if they are God's representatives then we too, in spite of all that was happening and still happens to us, we too are children of God. We too are those whom God has honored by asking us to be his partners. Partners in upsetting the powers and principalities. Partners in helping God to establish his kingdom. And God was saying: "Hey, don't go around trying to apologize for your existence, man. I didn't make a mistake creating you as who you are. You are not a faint copy, carbon copy of somebody else; you are an original." That was seeping through into our consciousnesses in ways that we were not always aware of, and the subversion had begun.

You see, as you very well know, one of the ways of helping to destroy a people is to tell them that they don't have a history, that they have no roots. They did it in many ways. One of them was writing history from the perspective of white people. Now we weren't over-bright, but this history of South Africa began to strike us as odd. We read about white colonists coming to our country in the 17th century. Whenever the Dutch or English colonists went over into black territory and got the blacks' cattle, the word used was that the colonists "captured" the cattle. But almost always when they wrote about a similar expedition on the part of the Xhosas, the Xhosas always "stole" the cattle. And we were very young, but I mean we began to scratch our heads. How come? These guys had no cattle when they came into our country. How then did they manage to have cattle which we would "steal" from them and they would be "capturing" from us?

"One of the ways of helping to destroy a people is to tell them that they don't have a history, that they have no roots."

But you see, if you tell something sufficiently often you come to believe it and those who listen to you perhaps also believe it. And you begin to gnaw away at their self-image and they begin to see themselves as you depict them. When you call them, as we used to be called "non-whites," "non-Europeans."

Words into Things

Those people who say that language is not important don't know what they are talking about. Those people who think that language is merely descriptive of reality don't know what they are talking about. We who have been victims of a process of denigration know that language is also creative: It brings about what it describes. If you say to people for long enough that they are non-this, non-the-other, it doesn't take very long before they begin to believe and speak of themselves also in negative terms. So that it becomes almost a kind of self-fulfilling prophecy.

It is actually quite wonderful, the kind of things that used to happen at home. Back in the old days they used to call us Natives, with a capital N. Now, that applied only to people with our color of skin. If you went to a white South African, born in the country, and you said innocently, "Excuse me, Ma'am, are you a native of these parts?" you would know very soon that you had committed the most awful *faux pas,* and you would wish that the earth would open up and swallow you. Because she certainly was not a "Native" of those parts.

They used to have extraordinary road signs which read, "Drive carefully, Natives cross here." Somebody changed the sign to read, rather hair-raisingly, "Drive carefully. Natives very cross here."

Rewriting History

They also wrote history in a way that made us not know huge chunks of our history. In South Africa, we knew hardly anything at all about the ancient kingdoms of West Africa. It is only in recent times that we began to realize Israel found its beginnings in Africa. It was only very recently that we began to know that in fact Christianity itself has had tremendous input from Africa, that Christian history has ancient, deep-lying roots in Africa. We didn't know this.

Now, my dear brothers and sisters, I come from a land where they ban all kinds of literature as being subversive. You are not allowed to read this and that and the other because it would put ideas in you heads. Our children are prevented from reading histories that will tell them about the French Revolution. It would put ideas into their heads— liberty, fraternity, equality—how can you speak about those things? The histories that our children have to study have been expurgated so that you don't see any references to the American War of Independence. But, we said to the government, you know, you are late. The book that you should have banned a long time ago is the Bible.

You know, long ago they used to say, "Well, you know the missionaries came to Africa and they had the Bible and we had the land. And then they said, 'Let us pray.' And when we opened our eyes, we had the Bible and they had the land." Well, sometimes people think that that was not a very fair exchange. I don't know, I don't know whether that is true because ultimately we have been given something which land would not have given us: the knowledge that we are those whom God has made in his image, those destined to be heirs of the kingdom.

Land in Flames

I came to this country three weeks ago. We should have come much earlier to the United States. We had to postpone our departure because of the upheaval in our land. We called an emergency meeting of our executive committee [of the South African Council of Churches] because we thought that our land was going up in flames. We called on the authorities to meet up with church leaders and see whether there was something that could be done to arrest what was happening and insure that our people were not going to be mowed down as they had been mowed down at Sharpeville in 1960 when 69 of our people, protesting peacefully against the pass laws, had been mowed down, and when incontrovertible evidence had shown that most of those 69 were shot in the back running away.

We wanted to insure too that our people were not going to be mowed down as our children had been mowed down in 1976. Then our children were protesting peacefully, singing in the streets, protesting inferior education meant to perpetuate us in an existence of serfdom and inequality. Our children protesting and over 500 people died as a result of Soweto's uprising in 1976. We didn't want to see that happen. We didn't want to see people being taken into jail and held without charges preferred against them and dying mysteriously in detention as it happened with Steve Biko. When Biko died the man who was then the minister of justice, so-called, was asked what he felt about the death and he said it left him cold.

So on this occasion, our committee said, let us visit the areas of unrest. We went to a black township called Wattville and we went into the home of an old lady and we said, "Can you tell us what happened?"

Black Children Treated as Animals

She said, "Yes, Bishop. My grandchildren were playing in the front of the house, in the yard. I look after my grandchildren and some children of our neighbors when their mothers have gone off to work. The police went past here chasing school children. They didn't find them. There was no riot happening at the time, and the police came down the street and swept past my house and they stopped. Bishop, I was sitting in the kitchen which is at the back of my house when one of my children rushed into the kitchen and said, 'Mommy, please come,' I rushed out. My grandson of six was lying just inside the front door. Shot in the back. Dead. Only six years old."

Now, even if there was a riot, what in the name of everything that is good could you say a six-year-old would do to police armed to the teeth? How do you manage to shoot a six-year-old in the back? The normal story that they will tell you is, "They were stone throwing and the police retaliated." The oldest of the children in that group could not have been more than 13 years of age. You shoot them, because when you look at them you don't see human beings. If those had been white children they would not have shot them, even under the greatest kind of provocation.

South Africa says, "Our economy is going to be based on cheap black labor and we can insure that that labor is cheap by separating off the men from their families and having them live in single-sex hostels for 11 months of the year. Therefore we can pay them as if they were single and the cost of production is decreased accordingly."

So those who invest in South Africa, invest in a system which we have described as being as evil, as un-Christian, as immoral as Communism ever was, as Nazism ever was. They invest in a system that depends on black misery and suffering. When some people suggest to them—I don't because I can't; if I stood up here and said that I support disinvestment it would be five years in jail so I am not talking about it—if someone else says to those who invest in South Africa, "Hey, why don't you pull out?" they will be the first to say, "You know, the people who will suffer the most if we pull out are blacks."

Baloney! For all these many years they have depended on black misery and suffering. What makes them suddenly become these wonderful altruists who care about black suffering? I am not a cynic. I am merely asking a question. . . .

Wonderful White People

These wonderful white people came to our country and out of a generosity that our people have, we welcomed them into our country. They were dying of scurvy on their way to the East and so they wanted fresh water and vegetables and things. You know, people said, "Okay, come on. We welcome you as our guests." Now they tell us, in our country, that we are no longer citizens of this country. They denationalized us. I carry a strange document for traveling around. It is not even a passport. Now, I am a South African of the golden sunshine, the gold, and the Krugerrand. My father was born in South Africa. My mother was born in South Africa, my mother's mother—you go right back. We belong here. Well then, there are some people who don't understand that. I carry this document for travel purposes. Inside here, where there is a place for nationality, you would think it would say "South Africa." This thing here says of my nationality, "Undeterminable at present." You might think I am making it up. "Undeterminable at present." They don't know where to slot me because they say South Africa is made up of several nations. The Xhosas are one nation; the Tswanas and so forth and so forth.

> "My grandson of six was lying just inside the front door. Shot in the back. Dead."

Now, the whites form one nation. We are not very subtle. A cabinet minister said to us, about us, "Well, the black Africans have not been included in the current constitutional proposals where Coloureds, people of mixed blood, and Indians and whites are now going to come together. The reason is that blacks are slow thinkers."

Among the whites there are French, English, German, you name it. Now we say, "Please just tell us how is it possible for whites of these disparate groups to come together and coalesce and be one nation? And we who are Africans are split up into all these different nations?"

No Political Rights

The purpose, obviously, is to turn us into aliens in the land of our birth. Because you see, when you are an alien, one thing you cannot claim is political rights.

So, when we stand up and say that this is un-Christian, they say, "Hey, you are mixing politics with religion." They tell us, "You are a Communist." Now maybe that sounds familiar. And then we ask, "Hey, which Bible do you read? Would you kindly tell us which Bible you read which would enable you to have this dichotomy?''

We don't read the same Bible. When did the people of Israel experience God for the first time as God? Did they experience God in worship? That is not what the Bible says. The Bible says the people of Israel experienced God when God performed a political act, helping rebel slaves escape out of bondage. And from that time on people said, ''Ah, this is the kind of God we have. A liberating God. A God who takes the side of the oppressed, of the hungry, of the exploited, of the weak.''

"The purpose. . . is to turn us into aliens in the land of our birth."

Which Bible do you read? Have you read Matthew, chapter 25? Jesus tells a strange parable there. He says, ''How is it going to be determined how you go to heaven or to the warmer place? Did you feed the hungry? Did you clothe the naked? Did you visit the sick? Did you visit those who are in prison?'' Jesus says, ''Inasmuch as you have done it to these you would have done it to me. So if you want to know where I am in South Africa, you go to the KTC squatter camp. That is where I am.''

A Strange Country

And so, let me finish, my friends, and say your country is a strange country. Let me be careful. I am a visitor here. Your country: When the Polish leader General Jaruzelski did something to Solidarity, your country, before you could say Jackie Robinson, applied sanctions against Poland.

And then the same kind of thing is done to black trade unionists in South Africa and you say Hey, what are you doing about that situation? They say, no, no, no. Sanctions don't work. Sanctions don't work. We must have a policy of constructive engagement. We must talk to these people and try to persuade them.

Your country is strange. There is a government, a legal, properly constituted government, in Nicaragua. That government is being attacked by people who in this country are called *contras*. They are ''liberation freedom fighters.'' And your government supports them with arms, and there is nothing said about violence. There is nothing said about terrorism.

And then in our country there is government, a minority government which excludes 73 percent of the people, and it claims it is a democracy. Our people from 1912 have sought to change that system by peaceful means. I indicated to you some of the things that happened when our people have tried to use peaceful means. And so, when our people are told that their organizations have become banned organizations, and they can no longer do anything

else, and they decide that they are going to fight for our freedom, your government says our freedom fighters are terrorists. And they tell us, violence never works.

And we say, What are you talking about? Your history! I mean, you are the last people to tell us about violence. You ought to be ashamed.

Now I want to ask you. Jesse Jackson and others have shown that you [black Americans] are a power to be reckoned with. Whatever your views may be of him, he has done a tremendous amount for black people, not just in this country but everywhere. Jesse has sought to place on the agenda something that would not have been discussed in this country: South Africa and the third world. Now my friends, I am saying to you, how is it possible that the Polish community in this country can have so much clout that the government here dare not, so they say, ignore what is happening in Poland? How come the Jewish community here has so much clout that your government is always on the side of Israel? How come when things happen in our country against black people, your government suddenly is all nice and sweet reasonableness. How come you don't have clout?

How come you think you have no clout? How come you allow the kinds of things that happen in South Africa to happen with the aid of your government?

We Depend on You

And so I end by saying: We depend on you. We depend on you because our liberation is your liberation. As long as we are unfree—to that extent you are going to be unfree in this country. And let me say to you, there is no doubt we are going to be free. Whether you help us or not. For the God whom we worship is the Exodus God, the God who leads his people always out of bondage into freedom. And so, St. Paul says, and there is a lovely chorus: If God be for us, If God be for us, If God be for us, who can be against us, who can be against us? And so, victory is ours in and through Him who died for us and if God is for us, who can be against us?

Bishop Desmond Tutu, 1984 Nobel Peace laureate, is general secretary of the South African Council of Churches. He is perhaps the most prominent anti-apartheid spokesman for his country. This viewpoint is part of an informal talk the bishop gave at the fourth national conference of Partners in Ecumenism (PIE) in Washington, DC.

"I consider Tutu's...equation of apartheid and Hitlerian holocaust a contemptible trivialization of the first magnitude."

viewpoint 114

Apartheid Is Improving

Otto Ulc

Clifton Wharton Jr. is chairman of the board of the Rockefeller Foundation, a director of the Ford Motor Co., and chancellor of the State University of New York. His essay, "U.S. Should Get Out of South Africa," appeared in *Newsday*....

The author concluded that apartheid "rivals in many respects the genocidal pogroms of Adolf Hitler," and that blacks "have been bound even more tightly with the barbed wire of apartheid."

According to Chancellor Wharton, for the millions of blacks not lucky enough to work for American firms, conditions are worse than ever. The obdurate Pretoria created phantom homelands and administers the legalized enslavement of 22 million blacks. Furthermore, Wharton charges, Reagan's policy of "constructive engagement" does not confront this atrocity and is a sham.

As Paul Johnson pointed out in his remarkable book, *Modern Times,* one of the most puzzling features of our modern era is aversion to facts, rejection of empirical evidence—an effort to theorize it out of existence.

Having had the unsolicited opportunity to experience a lifestyle under Nazi occupation and postwar Stalinism, after my disappearance from the cage I have engaged in some compensatory globe-trotting. Of the hundred or so countries visited I perhaps do understand some of them, and surely fail to comprehend others. The Republic of South Africa was on my itinerary in 1977 and 1979.

Decision to Visit South Africa

In 1984, after a thorough chat with my Eurasian wife and teenage son, we decided to spend a part of my sabbatical and a great deal of money to get to South Africa and see for ourselves the realm of genocidal demons. Some of the faculty colleagues

Otto Ulc, "Don't Believe Everything You Hear About South Africa," *Human Events,* May 25, 1985. Reprinted with permission.

diagnosed my plan as sheer irresponsibility. It was even suggested I consult a psychiatrist.

In addition to anticipated problems (i.e., marriage to a person of mixed race—inter-racial marriages being forbidden by law in South Africa), I was aware of stepping on a minefield with further explosives: What if I find something positive to say about the affairs in that country and about a salutary effect of Reagan's constructive engagement policy? Anything less than an unqualified condemnation seems tantamount to complicity, to endorsement of apartheid, an indelible blemish on one's reputation, possibly a peril to one's career. Quite a dilemma for a Czech by birth; we have avoided fighting since the 17th Century.

However, since Chancellor Wharton felt free to condemn the President of the United States, I may perhaps be permitted to report with impunity our findings, not entirely in accord with the Chancellor's assertions.

In Contact with Revolutionaries

In 60 days (September 1–October 30) we drove altogether 14,000 kilometers, from the Mozambique border in the east to the rather tranquil guerrilla war theater in northern Namibia. In Johannesburg we missed a bomb explosion by one hour. We contacted as many people as possible—revolutionaries and reactionaries, rural blacks in the arid Karoo region, influential Afrikaners on their palatial premises.

Not even once was my family subjected to anything that could be termed "racial prejudice"—be that in ordinary, "non-international" hotels, restaurants or whichever other situations of social contact. Nobody kicked out my wife from officially segregated premises (an experience with which she was quite familiar in the late '50s in the United States). Yes, in Transvaal and Orange Free State we were occasionally stared at, by whites and blacks alike, but these were curious rather than hostile stares.

I hasten to acknowledge that apartheid has not been abolished—not yet. But it has not remained the same, either.

A few years ago, the odious signs of racial segregation were the rule. Nowadays they are becoming an exception. We saw no such signs in Durban or in Cape Town; they do survive especially in smaller places.

"Bullying is counterproductive; it triggers a backlash to the benefit of racist reactionaries."

(Example: Rustenburg municipal campaign ground, sign "Whites Only." We checked in and next morning I inquired at the desk whether we had violated the law—and surreptitiously I taped the conversation. "No sir," an angelic blond lady assured me, "we even let in the Jews and the Greeks.")

Public Association of Races

At the time of my first visit in the RSA [Republic of South Africa], parks were segregated. In 1984, we saw whites and non-whites holding hands, strolling, some even in amorous embrace—thus in flagrant violation of apartheid statutes. Nobody yelled for the police. That was in Johannesburg, in Transvaal where race tensions are more acute than elsewhere.

In 1977, the government refused permission for a multiracial audience to attend in Durban the premiere of a play sponsored by the Progressive Reform party. I was there. In 1984, with my family and friends of various colors we went in Johannesburg to see a forcefully anti-apartheid drama, *Poppie*. The multi-racial audience applauded the black performers; the authorities did not interfere. According to a public opinion poll in October 1984, the percentage of Transvaalers who still insist on segregated "white only" beaches dropped from 51 per cent to 13 per cent. During our stay, integration of trains was introduced, albeit on a limited scale thus far.

Government More Liberal

The government set up a commission to scrap the Mixed Marriages Act and the repugnant Section 16 of the Immorality Act. In 1985, it was announced, South Africans of all races will be issued the same kind of identity documents—a practice common in most countries—thus abolishing the hated passbooks. The train is indeed rolling down the track, and, hopefully, it will not be derailed. The movement is visible to all willing to see.

In Mamelodi, an unattractive black suburb or Pretoria, I visited the campus of Vista, a new university concentrating on the badly needed

upgrading of black teachers. (The Vista project is quite unlike the little-respected black universities such as the University of the North, set up during the 1950s.)

Prof. E. R. Jenkins, campus director, a white liberal if there ever was one, described the changes in admission policy of non-white students to white universities.

Old rule: Each such application had to be sent to Pretoria for governmental approval. New rule: Pretoria finally abolished this practice and instead assigned quotas of the non-white contingent, leaving it up to the universities to administer the new program.

New reality: The universities refused to become an enforcing tool of the government's policy. Instead, qualified applicants regardless of race are being admitted—hence a practice that violates the law and the government looks the other way.

"Aren't these changes merely cosmetic?" I asked.

"It is the other way around," laughed Vista head Jenkins. "The cosmetic is still there—the change is behind it." He characterized P. W. Botha's rule as a "government by exception." Laws are being promulgated (e.g., quotas for university admission of non-whites) and the civil servants are being instructed to ignore them.

Private Catholic schools, in particular, we were told, ignore with impunity the apartheid vestiges. For example, in one such white school in a white suburb of Pretoria, 60 percent of the students are non-white. (Yet, in the same city, the facilities of the municipal library remain strictly segregated.)

Segregation Hurts the Economy

If for no other reason, segregation is to disappear because it hurts the economy and is too costly. In a Johannesburg skyscraper we visited a medical laboratory employing 250 people of five different racial categories. All share the same facilities. Who would want to pay for five cafeterias? Segregation has also become impossible to police. Of the estimated 8.7 million blacks living in white areas, some two million are there illegally.

"We are being crucified because apartheid still bears the 1948 number plate," complained Barend du Plessis, minister of finance (New York *Times,* Oct. 3, 1984) and pledged: "We have already undergone considerable change and will eventually end up without apartheid." Some even more outspoken Afrikaners claim that apartheid as such is dead—what matters now is to cope with De Tocqueville's wise warning that the greatest danger a bad regime faces is at the time of introducing good changes.

Well-Intentioned May Disagree

Well-intentioned people may disagree on a number of important issues.

Is participation in administering the black

townships a constructive thing or a sell-out? To boycott or not to boycott the new parliamentary arrangement (an echo of the dilemma the Socialists faced in pre-1917 Russia)? Some (e.g., the Labour party) consider participation as the best road toward betterment, others (e.g., the United Democratic Front) reject it out of hand.

Riots, urban violence, governmental repression in the Vaal Triangle: Was it triggered by the rent increase or by more fundamental grievances? Was the violence a spontaneous action of frustrated masses or a result of manipulation by a minority to terrorize the peaceful majority? Were the victims martyrs to a cause or a part of a mob, looting and burning mostly African and Indian property, blacks killing blacks, some hacked to pieces?

Homelands: Are these viable nation-state entities or a "great confidence trick," as Gatsha Buthelezi, the chief of the Zulu nation, put it? Unlike the green, fertile Zululand, the homelands are rather arid and undeveloped. Yet, some are more viable in economic terms than many member of the United Nations. Lebowa and Bophutatswana have rich mineral deposits—chromium, vanadium, platinum—valued in billions of dollars.

At any rate, when ever before has economic viability been considered a prerequisite for independence? The large, populous Transkei would promptly be recognized and welcomed by the international community if its parent had been Great Britain (i.e., as in the case of pathetically poor Lesotho) rather than South Africa.

Puppet States

In terms of per capital GNP, these puppet states are better off than 30, perhaps 40 recognized Third World countries—and Bophutatswanta is much better off (a fact of life readily acknowledged by the Botswanese people). Its president, Lucas Mangope, has the reputation of a competent, honest leader, in contrast to Lennox Sebe, the miserable, corrupt despot in Ciskei.

"We don't want apartheid and we want to show the world that if we stand together, we can bring about its downfall and lead society on the road to a Federal Republic of South Africa," vowed Cedric Phatudi, chief minister of Lebowa. Strange words for a "puppet".

The defenders of government policies confronted me with arguments such as: "You demand from us a standard of behavior that you do not expect from the rest of Africa. We, the Boers, never conquered any nation, we have no blood on our hands. We saved the Ndebele people from extermination by the Zulus. We have no ties to Europe."

But the apartheid system they do have on their hands.

"It is not our international responsibility to commit national suicide. One man, one vote. Yes—once.

Which example of African democracy are we supposed to follow?"

Exceptionally difficult to say. The record is rather dismal.

Even the determined critics of apartheid stressed the heterogeneity of South African society in which the First World and the Third World exist side by side, in which half of the black people live tribally with almost no contacts with the whites.

Thus far the democratic form of government proved to be a thoroughly unsuitable Western import. Hence, why impose on South Africa a device that failed in the rest of Africa? A unitary, parliamentary structure of the Western type will end in a bloodbath. It is stupid, to say the least, to accord political rights to peoples with solely tribal loyalties, I was told over and over.

Divest or not to divest? Thus far the record of punitive measures—boycotts and sanctions—has not provided much evidence as to their effectiveness. For example, instead of being prevented access to weaponry, the country has become an exporter of arms. Boycott, however, worked very well in sports: it is now organized on a non-racial basis (an accomplishment not many human rights advocates are prepared to acknowledge).

Danger in Compromising Success

But, as Harry Oppenheimer (in his address to the Foreign Policy Association in New York in October 1984) pointed out, there is a danger in compromising the success of the past. Bullying is counter-productive; it triggers a backlash to the benefit of racist reactionaries. For example, the clumsy meddling of Carter's Administration alienated the opposition Progressive Federal party and ushered in a period of sterile hostility.

"In . . . racist RSA the oppressed black majority has on average a higher standard of living than do their liberated brethren in the rest of Africa."

Not even the most ardent champions of divestment deny that the introduction of the so-called "Sullivan Principles" (desegregation in the work-place, equality of pay, also financial aid to black communities) have indeed worked to the benefit of the black workers. Not all U.S. companies signed the pledge of adherence to these principles; of those who signed up, some (e.g., Ford, IBM, Exxon) receive high grades for compliance, others receive failing grades.

The divestment lobby has always claimed it is acting on behalf of the south African black majority. Well, the feeling of the majority did pop up in a solid survey: 75 per cent respondents rejected withdrawal of foreign capital and trade boycotts as a strategy for their liberation (Center for Applied Social Sciences poll, September 1984).

Putting aside the practicality of withdrawing funds and plants (the U.S. is not the largest investor; its place will be filled by investment money from Europe and Asia); I have to pause and contemplate the elitist, truly Leninist posture of the divestment advocates. Some blacks will suffer, but it is a price gladly to be paid. Hunger performs a useful function, so opined 22-year-old Vladimir I. Uljanov when opposing famine relief.

Divestment Immoral

Alan Paton, hardly a novice to the cause of justice in his native South Africa, in response to Desmond Tutu, wrote: "I do not understand how your Christian conscience allows you to advocate disinvestment. I think your morality is as confused as was the morality of the church in the Inquisition, or the morality of Dr. Verwoerd in his utopian dreams" (*Sunday Times*, Johannesburg, Oct. 21, 1984).

"The practitioners of selective indignation protest the misdeeds of the South African government but remain dead silent about manifold outrages in the Third World orbit."

Two weeks later, in the same paper, Paton added: "I will never give any support to any campaign that will put men out of jobs—not even if they promised me that it would bring Chernenko down. Or Reagan. Or P. W. Botha." In short, a hopeless humanist. "Masses are irrelevant!" so I was told by committed elitist revolutionaries at a champagne-*cum*-caviar underground soiree in the best Johannesburg suburbia.

Chancellor Wharton repeats the frequently heard assertion that millions upon millions of black South Africans are worse off today than a few years ago, that significant impoverishment of most blacks took place, that black semi-slave labor languishes in South African mines.

According to the Dec. 24, 1984, issue of *Time*, while real income for whites has declined during the 1970s the average income has climbed by more than 50 per cent to $1,560.

Yet, the average income of South African whites is still 13 times higher than that of the blacks. How fast and how much will the sharing of wealth proceed? The envy and resentment of the economic well-being of the whites (and Indians) is considerable.

The economy is in recession, the most severe in half a century. Partly the government is to be blamed

(excessive regulatory practices, choking the economy), partly it is the result of forces beyond control: the price of gold, the main source of foreign currency earnings, continues to fall. The rains do not. South Africa experiences the most severe drought in half a century.

Since we do not blame the lack of precipitation in Mozambique on Marxism, we surely cannot blame the same state of arid affairs in the Republic of South Africa on apartheid. Wherever we went, drought was the most frequent topic of discussion. In Botswana, we were told, 80 per cent of cattle—the main source of wealth—perished. The mood is gloomy in all the neighborhood regardless of political stripes.

Returning to the Leninist principle of desirable suffering—of others: To denounce the employment of foreign labor as semi-slavery is one thing, to lose such a job is a different matter. Robert Mugabe raised such accusations and Pretoria responded by terminating the contracts of the Zimbabweans, thus liberated, unemployed and perhaps unemployable.

In undoubtedly racist RSA the oppressed black majority has on average a higher standard of living than do their liberated brethren in the rest of Africa: better housing, schools and health care. (According to the New York *Times*, Dec. 27, 1981, black welders in the RSA reportedly make more money than white welders in Great Britain.) Therefore, the oppressed are not fleeing the inferno; the hungry ones are trying to get in.

Five out of six Lesotho males work in the RSA. Since divestment would cast a long shadow, I brought up in discussions in Lesotho the efforts of their avowed overseas friends. The response was predictable and not too friendly.

The RSA is the major economic power on the continent and the major source of critical minerals in the world. Trade sanctions and punitive measures were forcefully imposed by the United Nations, but trade between the RSA and the rest of Africa continues to boom: it more than doubled in the last five years. . . .

Possibility of City-States

The millions of the blacks living outside the tribal homelands should be drawn into regional and national administration along with the whites, Indians and Cape Coloreds. A thought is also given to a concept of City-States, such as Soweto, with or without ties to any homeland, a recipe perhaps as impractical as the importation of Westminster democracy.

Enter Bishop Desmond Tutu, the momentary darling of the Western media, the recipient of a standing ovation on Capitol Hill in Washington, and of the Nobel Peace Prize in Oslo (thus joining the co-laureates such as Henry Kissinger and Le Duc Tho for ushering in peace and prosperity in Vietnam).

If contribution to the cause of civil rights was the

main criterion, Chief Buthelezi and Helen Suzman were surely more worthy Nobel Prize candidates. Cleric Tutu—as representative of the South African blacks, as say, William Sloane Coffin is a typical spokesman for white American Christians—is met with less enthusiasm in circles familiar with his record. His dovish, sanctimonious pronunciations abroad do not quite match with his performance on home turf.

Tutu tends to damage good causes with huge exaggerations: "Tutumuchism," so it is called in South Africa. In London, en route to the Scandinavian festivities, the bishop asserted that the blacks in his country would prefer a Soviet type of communism to apartheid. While I sincerely would wish various West Europeans and North Americans, a portion of our SUNY Binghamton faculty included, the lifelong opportunity to savor all the flavors of Soviet scientific socialism, I would not wish it on the South African blacks. They deserve better.

According to laureate Tutu, civil rights fare better in the USSR than in the RSA. When will laureate Andrei Sakharov pop up in the West, vilifying the Soviet government and returning home with impunity?

A Contemptible Trivialization

As a former *Untermensch* in the Third Reich I consider Tutu's—and not only Tutu's—equation of apartheid and Hitlerian holocaust a contemptible trivialization of the first magnitude. Many things, of course, are comparable—both, a stick and a nuclear bomb, are weapons: the difference is merely quantitative. Genocide in South Africa? In the last 30 years, mortality of black children below the age of five dropped by two-thirds, not quite the experience of Jewish children during the Final Solution.

"In the last 30 years, mortality of black children below the age of five dropped by two-thirds."

The same critics of President Reagan's policy of constructive engagement vis-a-vis South Africa condemn him for his lack of constructive engagement vis-a-vis the Soviet Union. Any volunteers on U.S. campuses to march in protest of the Soviet invasion of Afghanistan? So far, over three million refugees, hundreds of thousands killed, wounded, maimed.

SUNY Binghamton signed, or is about to sign, an exchange cooperative agreement with Indonesia. The Indonesian government, some of us surely still remember, has been engaged for many years in the destruction of the indigenous way of life of the Melanesian population in West Irian, and in a genuine genocidal slaughter in East Timor. But SUNY Binghamton prefers to protest the Marriott catering service at the Johannesburg airport.

Evidently, morality is easily divisible. Is it also perhaps racially tainted? The practitioners of selective indignation protest the misdeeds of the South African government but remain dead silent about manifold outrages in the Third World orbit. In my way of thinking, they put the authenticity of their wrath into jeopardy; they indeed do expect and demand higher standards of civilized behavior on the part of the white folk. Some doubts do indeed creep into the minds of those not sufficiently fortified with the ideological certitudes of the day.

To those rushing to condemn me on account of ignorance, arrogance, or racial insensitivity, I wish to point out that as in the case of charity, racial tolerance begins at home. I have practiced it in matrimonial harmony for 20 years.

Otto Ulc is a professor of political science at the State University of New York at Binghamton. A native of Czechoslovakia and the author of several books, he visited South Africa in September and October of 1984 together with his wife.

"South Africa is moving... toward a state of war in which foreign investment strengthens the strategic position of one side."

Disinvestment Would Aid South African Blacks

James North

South African president P. W. Botha has long been known as a man with a volatile temper. But three years ago he issued a warning to the anti-apartheid forces that went beyond his usual outbursts. In a major speech opening parliament, he said, "Something will happen in South Africa that the proponents of violence cannot even dream of. They don't know what they are going to reap." Later he added even more chillingly, "A big silence and desolation will come over many parts of South Africa."

In the past six months, the country's growing internal violence has brought Botha's threat closer to reality. A brief lull in the nationwide unrest ended in late February, when the police opened fire at the crossroads squatter camp near Cape Town. Since September, more than 200 people have been killed, and another 3,000 arrested—including nine prominent black political and labor leaders who will be tried for treason and who could face the death penalty. Some 500,000 black workers staged a two-day general strike in November, the largest in history, and another 400,000 black students have boycotted classes to protest their segregated "gutter education." The uprising is a bitter, convincing repudiation of the "reform" proposals that Pretoria put forward with much fanfare last year. South Africa is sliding remorselessly toward the same violence that already prevails in Namibia, its colony to the north, where the apartheid army is fighting a full-scale guerilla war that may already have killed 10,000 people.

No Reforms Made in Apartheid

Steadily increasing turbulence is the reality against which foreign investment and bank loans to South Africa must be considered. Those who defend

James North, "The Case for Cutting Off South Africa: Divestment Imperative," *The New Republic*, March 25, 1985. Reprinted by permission of THE NEW REPUBLIC, © 1985, The New Republic, Inc.

economic involvement attempt to portray a nation moving toward genuine reform; investments, they argue, help this evolutionary process by promoting economic growth and more enlightened racial practices. This assertion, which has been made for more than 20 years, is today hollower than ever. South Africa is moving in the opposite direction, toward a state of war in which foreign investment strengthens the strategic position of one side.

Up-to-date Western technology is probably the most vital benefit that the economic links provide to Botha's government. The regime has taken advantage of the Reagan administration's relaxed restrictions on sensitive exports, and has acquired powerful Control Data and Sperry computers, which are functioning in military-related enterprises. The three huge, futuristic Sasol plants that convert coal into oil, which South Africa needs desperately, are being built partly by Fluor, another U.S. corporation. American contractors are also working under shadowy circumstances in the nuclear industry. Bank loans to South Africa have been used, directly or indirectly, to finance a massive military buildup. The International Monetary Fund's $1.1 billion loan two years ago exactly equaled the increase in military spending from 1980 to 1982.

America Encourages Whites

Western economic involvement also helps to maintain the morale of the majority of the white people who still support apartheid. Whites are by now used to the feeble, ritual criticisms of their system by Western governments. But they are surrounded by vivid evidence of the American economic stake in apartheid, including Ford and Chevrolet autos, branches of Holiday Inns, outposts of Colonel Sanders, even Kellogg's Corn Flakes. All of this encourages them to believe that America will continue to stand by them as the war widens.

In the United States, the diminishing number of

people who support investment argue that black South Africans actually want continued economic links. The State Department has taken to quoting a survey by a white South African academic that purportedly shows that three-quarters of blacks support investment. The State Department fails to note that South Africa is a police state, and that it is a crime to advocate disinvestment. A few years back, Bishop Tutu was forbidden to travel outside the country after he hinted that he favored limited economic pressure. If he had been a less prominent figure, the security police doubtless would have been harder on him.

"South Africa is heading deeper into a bloody civil war whether there are sanctions or not."

The popular movements with bases outside the country, principally the African National Congress, have called for sanctions for decades. Nelson Mandela, the ANC leader who has been imprisoned for 20 years, is the most popular man in the country, and would be the most likely president of a nonracial, democratic South Africa. Those movements that operate openly inside, such as the United Democratic Front, a coalition of 600 community organizations, unions, and other groups representing 1.5 million people, have to be circumspect, but they privately favor increased economic pressure as well. Bishop Tutu, who enjoys greater immunity after winning the Nobel Peace Prize, says he will publicly advocate sanctions if there is no genuine change within 18 to 24 months. Zulu chief Gatsha Buthelezi is the only black leader with any appreciable following who still opposes sanctions; his support (which has been dwindling) is due largely to his resistance to Pretoria's plans to strip Zulu-speaking South Africans of their citizenship as part of the notorious Bantustan policy, rather than to stand on foreign investment.

Black South Africans recognize that the argument that U.S. companies improve conditions for the 70,000 black people they employ is exaggerated. It has been eight years since the Reverend Leon Sullivan introduced his code for the 350 U.S. corporations that do business there. The Sullivan Code requires desegragated canteens and restrooms in the work place and other mild changes. Only about one-third of all the enterprises have even bothered to sign the code, and not all of the signers comply with it.

Some Americans who lean toward disinvestment assume it will cause blacks to suffer more than in the short run; they hesitate before what they regard as a problematic moral decision. But black South Africans and the whites who support them have made that difficult choice already. They will continue their resistance, despite the risk of even greater anguish. South Africa is heading deeper into a bloody civil war whether there are sanctions or not. Chief Albert Lutuli, who in 1960 was the first black South African to win the Nobel Peace Prize, wrote then: "The economic boycot of South Africa will entail undoubted hardship for Africans. We do not doubt that. But if it is a method which shortens the day of bloodshed, the suffering to us will be a price we are willing to pay. In any case, we suffer already."

American Protest Buoys Black South Africans

In America, disinvestment has spread far beyond the college campuses where it first became an issue. Already five states and many cities, including New York, Boston, and Philadelphia, have passed disinvestment legislation. But even the staunchest advocates realize it will not happen soon. This spring Congress will consider legislation on economic sanctions. The proposed laws still fall short of a total economic quarantine, though they are stiffer than previous efforts that failed to pass. They ban new investment, bank loans to government institutions, and the importing of the gold coins called Krugerrands. As an unprecedented protest campaign against apartheid spreads across America, the chance for passage seems good.

Even such part-way pressures are enormously helpful. Protest here receives a great deal of publicity inside South Africa. When Senator Lowell Weicker was arrested in front of the embassy in Washington, the story was on the front pages in Johannesburg. Such news shakes the confidence of the government and its supporters. But there are more tangible benefits as well. In 1974 the United Mine Workers protested to the U.S. Commission of Customs that South African coal was produced by "slave labor" and should not be imported; and dockworkers in Mobile, Alabama, refused to unload the coal. The apartheid regime moved quickly, repealing some legislation under which black workers who quit their jobs without permission could be tried as criminals. There had been 17,000 prosecutions under the laws the previous year.

Economic Pressure

Since then, the deepening American economic involvement in South Africa has made that government even more vulnerable to pressure. In December the regime released 16 detained union leaders the same day the protests in Washington had compelled Ronald Reagan to meet with Bishop Tutu. No doubt Pretoria would prefer to dispense with the remnants of the independent judicial system and crush the labor unions and the opposition English-language press. The foreign vigilance has helped keep open at least some political space, and has prevented more people from being imprisoned or murdered.

Economic pressure from overseas can help restrain the regime's even more deadly policies. Wretched health conditions in the poor, overcrowded Bantustans, where more than half of all black people are required to live, have been worsened by the continent-wide drought. These people, whom the regime has called "superfluous," are disproportionately the young, the old, and the ill. Infant mortality rates in the Bantustans, which form an archipelago of misery scattered around the nation's periphery, are already higher than in even the poorest independent countries in the rest of Africa. Nearly three million blacks under 15 suffer from malnutrition. One-quarter of black children born in the Bantustans die before their first birthday. Even modest changes in the Bantustan system could mean the difference between life and death for thousands.

Economic Sanctions a Necessity

Economic sanctions are the last chance to end the violence spreading across southern Africa. Although it may seem paradoxical, disinvestment would also be in the best long-term interests of those South Africans, nearly all of them white, who continue to support apartheid. In part, they fight because they are convinced that defeat will mean their violent expulsion from Africa. In fact, the African National Congress, the leading liberation movement, insists that "South Africa belongs to all who live in it, black and white." But so far, white South Africans have had little inducement to reexamine their fearful and mistaken views, to learn that their fellow Africans are not the threat that they imagine. Increased economic pressure will moderate their intransigence, and improve the prospects for genuine negotiations.

"Economic sanctions are the last chance to end the violence spreading across southern Africa."

The most recent protests here in America have forced Botha to make some concessions, proving again that pressure from outside is more than simply a moral gesture. South Africa announced that it will suspend forced resettlement, a policy under which 3.5 million people have been dumped into the Bantustans. Up to one million more people who were scheduled for deportation have gained a reprieve. The regime also dropped plans to move 125,000 people from three black ghettos in Cape Town. These moves still leave the basic apartheid system intact. But they are promising signs that even more pressure, along with the courageous resistance inside the country, could force more substantive changes.

It is time the South African crisis stopped being a left vs. right issue here in America. Thirty-five Republican representatives recently broke with the administration by openly threatening Pretoria that they might support sanctions. The letter they released received a great deal of attention inside South Africa, and it did more good than four years of the Reagan administration's "constructive" whispering in P.W. Botha's ear. Americans of all political persuasions are starting to realize that there is a terrifying sense of urgency about South Africa's slide toward the edge. A recent Carnegie Endowment study speculated that the regime could have already stockpiled "enough material for between 15 and 25 nuclear explosives of the size used on Hiroshima." And where else in the world does a national leader threaten his own people with atomic weapons or something similarly catastrophic?

James North spent four years traveling throughout southern Africa. He is the author of Freedom Rising.

"Disinvestment would lead...toward the diminution of black rights rather than their expansion."

Disinvestment Would Hurt South African Blacks

The Lincoln Review

The record of many of those who are urging revolution in South Africa leads to the conclusion that they would like to inflict upon that country a system far more oppressive than the one it has now. And a fact which is largely ignored in the current debate is that the current system has undergone dramatic change in recent years—in the direction of a more open and equitable society.

South Africa is a society in the midst of peaceful evolution which its critics tend to ignore almost completely. They treat South Africa as if it were an intransigent, unchanging society committed to the maintenance of the apartheid policies of the past. In order to create such an unrealistic and untruthful picture, they have overlooked more than a decade of forward movement. Consider the following examples:

• In November, 1983, South African voters overwhelmingly endorsed a new constitution which brought non-whites, Indians and members of the Colored (mixed race) group into the political process for the first time. While this reform falls short of the equality which blacks seek, it represents a further deterioration of the apartheid system and a move in the direction of a multi-racial society. *The Economist* of London pointed out that, "There have been signs that classical apartheid is weakening under the pressure of economic change. Job reservation has all but collapsed. Some bits of 'petty' apartheid have been dismantled. Strengthened by overwhelming white support for the new constitution...Mr. Botha has set up a cabinet committee on new constitutional arrangements for urban blacks. Black unions are flourishing."

Jobs Opened to Whites and Blacks

• No longer is there legislation reserving certain jobs and occupations for whites. Blacks now have the right to organize labor unions. Per capita income figures for blacks and other non-whites in South Africa now range from two to five times higher than those of blacks in independent black countries. This explains why one million "guest workers" from neighboring countries choose to work in South Africa. Since 1970, the real earnings of non-white workers in industry and mining have been rising more sharply and more steadily than those of white workers. Between 1970 and 1979, the wage gap narrowed in all economic sectors. Real wages for blacks tripled between 1970 and 1979.

• Blacks in cities and suburbs now have the right to buy their own homes and the government has launched a massive electrification program in Soweto, the large black township outside of Johannesburg. Etienne Van Loggerenberg of Rand Afrikaans University estimates that in the five years prior to 1982, Soweto household incomes increased by 50 per cent. Soweto's disposable income will soon overtake that of its parent city. In 1970, said economist Arnt Spandau, the whites' share of total personal incomes in South Africa was 75 per cent compared to 25 per cent for non-whites. By 1980 the proportion had changed to 60 and 40 per cent.

• Stellenbosch University, the leading Afrikaans-language university, now enrolls black students for all post-graduate courses and for undergraduate courses that are not offered at South Africa's three black universities, and two separate universities for Indians and the Colored community. When this decision was made in 1977, Humphrey Taylor wrote in the *Christian Science Monitor:* "Steeped in tradition by its very surroundings, Stellenbosch University has also been steeped in an atmosphere of racial exclusivity as well. Every one of its 10,000 students is white. The decision to open the door to black students is a complete reversal of original National Party apartheid policy." Even before the Stellenbosch decision, major English-language universities such as

The Lincoln Review, "Disinvestment Would Hurt Black South Africans, the Very People It Is Meant to Help," Winter, 1985. Reprinted with permission.

Cape Town and Witwatersrand already enrolled about 500 black students each.

• In February, 1985, the government announced that it will open 44 business districts to merchants of all races, changing rules that have segregated black and white traders for more than 300 years. At the same time, South African state radio said that the country's race and sex laws—which ban marriage and sex between people of different races—had come to be seen as racially arrogant and "gratuitously offensive" and it would be a logical advance to review them. The South African Government also announced that it was suspending the forced resettlement policy.

New Government Benefits All Races

We could fill pages with reports of affirmative change taking place in South Africa. All of this means that there is, indeed, movement in the right direction—peacefully, in an evolutionary manner, benefiting South Africans of all races.

If we truly seek to improve race relations in that country—which is surely a legitimate goal for men and women of good will in the United States—what is the proper course for us to take? Is it to ignore the worthwhile changes already under way and urge the economic isolation of a government which is itself embarked upon change? Is it to support violent revolution which would turn South Africa into another Angola or Ethiopia, in which all citizens, black and white alike, would have fewer rights and freedoms than they do now?

The answer to these questions should clearly be: No! Yet, disinvestment would lead in precisely that direction, toward the diminution of black rights rather than their expansion.

"No longer is there legislation reserving certain jobs and occupations for whites."

There are some black spokesmen in South Africa who support disinvestment. These, however, are largely an unrepresentative fringe of radicals who seek violent revolution. The overwhelming majority of black South Africans—whose opinions and interests seem of little concern to TransAfrica and its friends in the anti-apartheid movement—want closer economic ties with the United States. They understand that such ties, and an expanding South African economy, are their best hope for progress.

In an effort to explore "the relationships between political attitudes and industrial issues among blacks in South Africa," the U.S. Department of State commissioned the highly regarded Centre for Applied Social Sciences at the University of Natal to undertake research into the attitudes of black

workers. The findings, described by Professor Lawrence Schlemmer who heads the Centre, as "remarkable," found that three-quarters of South Africa's black production workers support foreign investment in South Africa and reject disinvestment and boycott as a strategy for improving conditions.

The main question provided two options. Overseas peoples, banks and companies should either (1) "Stop buying South African goods and stop sending money to build factories in South Africa so as to frighten the South African government into getting rid of apartheid" or (2) "Continue to buy South African goods to send money to build factories because it makes jobs for all people in South Africa."

Seventy five per cent of those polled supported the second option. Less than 25 per cent supported disinvestment.

Blacks Oppose Disinvestment

Black leaders have been vocal in their opposition to disinvestment. Llewellyn Mehlomakulu, a prominent black banker from Soweto, urges American business and industry to continue its role in South Africa, which he says is an affirmative one with regard to blacks. He states: "The view of the South African black silent majority is never given the same kind of publicity as the pro-disinvestment viewpoint. The majority of blacks in South Africa is for continuing U.S. business involvement providing that it contributes to evolutionary change. When Polaroid was under pressure to withdraw from South Africa, for example, the representatives of Polaroid workers came to me and said that none of them were in favor of Polaroid or other foreign companies pulling out."

Mehlomakulu said: "In 1971, I was in the U.S. and I met with Roy Wilkins, then leader of the NAACP. He visited South Africa and said that U.S. investment and involvement was desirable. The image of American companies is good. They contribute to evolutionary change by doing things contrary to apartheid. They have integrated facilities and give equal pay for equal work. All justice-loving people understand that apartheid is not acceptable. But those who advocate business withdrawal and those who urge continued U.S. involvement differ on strategy....If the U.S. pulled out, you would lose your leverage for change."

Lucy Mvubelo, one of South Africa's most prominent black labor leaders, who serves as general secretary of the National Council of Clothing Workers and vice president of the Trade Union Council of South Africa, declares: "Those in our country who urge a boycott of South African goods and the disinvestment of Western capital are simply a small fringe of desperate revolutionaries. They realize that the basic conditions from which revolution can rise does not exist, thus the world must create it. Who will suffer? Clearly the greatest hardship would fall on my people, the black people. They will be the first to lose their jobs. They will be left to die of starvation. They will be the first to be killed in a revolution."

Disinvestment Will Make Things Worse

Councillor S.I.P. Kgama, a prominent black leader who founded the Urban Councillors Association of South Africa and now serves as president of the Dobsonville Council, says that he is totally against disinvestment: "Any such policy will cost us jobs. At the present time, there are 10 blacks seeking every job which comes available. Those who advocate disinvestment want to make things worse so that the people will be radicalized. But history shows us that power gained by violence is never freedom. It becomes a new kind of oppression." . . .

"We could fill pages with reports of affirmative change taking place in South Africa."

Those who truly seek a better and more equitable society in South Africa should re-think their support for disinvestment. Such a policy would defeat the very values it is meant to advance—would hurt the very people it is meant to help.

The Lincoln Review *is a quarterly publication published by the Lincoln Institute for Research and Education.*

"Multinational corporations in South Africa...can be a major force in the liberation of that country's black population."

US Corporations Can Change Apartheid

Leon H. Sullivan and William J. Choyke

Editor's note: This viewpoint is taken from two articles. The first is by Leon H. Sullivan. The second viewpoint is by William J. Choyke.

I

Multinational corporations in South Africa, along with other parties, can be a major force in the liberation of that country's black population. However, in order for this to happen U.S. companies and other foreign firms operating there must be pushed to the utmost to eliminate all racial discrimination in their operations, and to use their great strength to help persuade the South African government to end all apartheid laws. Corporations that fail to do so should be compelled to leave South Africa because they have no moral justification for remaining.

Corporate responsibility is not the total solution to the problem. Apartheid is the most racist and ruthless system on Earth, and its destruction will require the combined efforts of big business, unions, churches, governments, world public opinion and, most of all, the courageous efforts of those within the country. But the corporations can and should play a major role in the effort because they have been the main beneficiaries of the injustices, and they have a duty to help end them.

U.S. companies, in particular, should set the example. This can be done, among other things, through full adherence to the Sullivan Principles. The principles are an equal-rights code for corporation conduct in South Africa. They were initiated eight years ago, and are the most stringent measurement for corporate equal-rights responsibility in the world today.

Essentially the principles call for an end to all

discrimination against blacks in the workplace: equal pay for equal work, and the training and elevation of blacks in large numbers to supervisory and administrative jobs—including black supervision over whites. They also call for extensive aid to housing, health and other community programs; the recognition of representative independent free black trade unions that empower the black worker, who is the greatest hope for peaceful change in South Africa, and major emphasis on education for the black population, without which political apartheid will one day become economic apartheid.

A new, tougher version of the principles also requires U.S. companies to actively support the freedom of blacks to work or live where they choose, as well as the abolition of apartheid. This means that U.S. companies must use their power to work for the end of influx control, forced removals, detention without trial and passbook requirements so that blacks may gain full citizenship rights and equal participation in the political process.

The Sullivan Principles are working. As a result of the principles, U.S. plants are desegregated and black workers are beginning to receive equal pay for equal work. Blacks are being elevated to administrative and supervisory jobs, supervising whites and receiving training in technical skills, and black trade unions are being recognized. Schools, housing developments and medical facilities are being built, health programs are being initiated and thousands of young people are receiving better educations.

A Catalyst for Change

The effect of the principles also goes far beyond those things and beyond the opportunities that are provided for the limited number of blacks—less than 1% of the total black work force—employed by U.S. companies. The principles are a catalyst for change, and are affecting conditions for black workers throughout the country. They act as a lever on other companies. A group of South African companies employing a million workers, mostly blacks, are now adhering to the principles. The principles have started a revolution in industrial race relations across South Africa. They also have become a platform for many in South Africa who argue for equal rights in government and other places.

But far more must be done by U.S. and foreign firms—and much, much faster. Mounting protests and turmoil within South Africa make fundamental change urgent if the country is to avoid a bloodbath. The pace of change is far too slow. The corporations in South Africa are powerful, and most become "activists" in the struggle. One thousand international corporations in South Africa practicing equal rights and taking firm stands against apartheid would make a dramatic difference in helping bring about the dismantling of that brutal system. Companies must be pushed harder for faster results.

Unfortunately, more than 100 U.S. companies in South Africa still do not support the principles, and some that claim to be supporters are dragging their feet. *All* U.S. companies should fully implement the principles, and those that fail to do so should be pressured to leave South Africa through total divestment actions, stockholder resolutions, boycotts or other means.

Congress should make the newly toughened amplified principles mandatory for all American companies in South Africa, backed by embargoes, sanctions and other penalties for non-compliance. I would rather see 50 U.S. companies remain in South Africa aggressively promoting equal rights, and actively opposing apartheid, more than 300 firms using the Sullivan Principles as camouflage for business as usual.

US Companies Must Shape Up

U.S. companies must shape up or leave. Foreign corporations that do business in both the United States and South Africa should be required to follow stringent equal-rights principles in South Africa, or face severe U.S. import restraints. These companies also must be pressured by their own citizens and governments to aggressively oppose apartheid. Unfortunately, European companies are lagging well behind American firms, and the Japanese are doing nothing. South Africa is the place for the corporations of the world to demonstrate a concern for justice and humanity. The enemy of capitalism is not communism, but the selfishness of capitalism. It is time that big business showed another side to the world.

II

Before pop singer Michael Jackson completes his schedule for his tour of the United States, he should do America a favor and add one more stop—Soweto, the largest black township in South Africa.

In doing so, he would send a message to both the white and black populations of the only nation still racially segregated by law. The message to the blacks would be that the United States has not forsaken them, despite the widespread perception to that effect. The message to the whites would be that the United States rejects the highly emotional appeal by some Americans and South Africans for American disinvestment and a reduction in ties. Rather, we would be looking forward to improving relations between our two countries—as long as that included communicating with leaders of South Africa's black community.

A Jackson trip to Soweto would also signal a significant shift in how the American Government approaches South African apartheid. While their rhetoric has differed—Ronald Reagan sounds much more conciliatory—the Carter and Reagan Administrations have done little to encourage real change within South Africa.

US Businesses Are Trailblazers

Both have relied on American business to press for reform. And indeed, American companies in South Africa have been trailblazers in desegrating work facilities, providing equal pay for equal work, promoting blacks to supervisory capacities and contributing to schools and other community facilities. Many of the companies that have introduced these reforms have done so in compliance with the widely respected Sullivan code, a set of six voluntary principles for employment practices, named after its originator, the Rev. Leon Sullivan of Philadelphia.

But even the Sullivan principles have had a limited effect: Less than one half of the estimated 300 American companies in South Africa have signed the code, prompting the House of Representatives to include similar principles in the Export Administration Act, which is now in a House-Senate conference.

"American companies ought to become part and parcel of the whole movement of political, sociological reform in this country."

Yet another American businesman's project was the establishment of the Pace Commercial College, for high-school aged students in Soweto. A sparkling three-year-old institution financed through the American Chamber of Commerce of South Africa, it probably offers the best business education that American money can buy.

But the college, too, is a limited effort. For one thing, it provides little mixing of the races. All 500 students are black. For another, it does little to raise the political consciousness of its students and offers no courses in political science. This may not be surprising for a business college financed by foreign corporations, but it leaves a big gap in the education of many young South Africans. Asked what she thinks about the apartheid system, 16-year-old Pace student Sarah Dibetso, who aspires to become a bank manager, replied: "I never thought that much about it."

The problem is that, for all their good will, American companies are hardly in a position to prod the South African Government to repeal the laws that implement apartheid. This has prompted many liberal and labor leaders in South Africa to question whether American companies do not in fact contribute to apartheid.

"The United States should try a policy of enlightened engagement with South Africa."

Talking about the Pace Commercial College, Piroshaw Camay, general secretary of the Council of Unions of South Africa, noted: "These projects are only ameliorating the fact of apartheid, and in a sense perpetuating apartheid by keeping things separate. If there is a black school in a black community, what does that mean? That is apartheid. If they want to do something for change, bring the managing directors' kids in contact with black school kids."

Disinvestment Would Be Devastating

A number of black leaders would like to see American businessmen playing a more active role. Percy Quboza, one of the country's most prominent black journalists, argues that: "American companies ought to become part and parcel of the whole movement of political, sociological reform in this country." He also disputes the view, held by many concerned Americans, that the best way for American companies to fight apartheid is to withdraw from South Africa altogether: "Now this to me is a very strange way of bringing about peaceful change." He argues that disinvestment would cause "a massive economic destabilization" and would hasten "the day when a black-white confrontation becomes a reality."

Instead of requiring American multinationals to withdraw, Washington should strengthen ties in South Africa, particularly in black areas like Soweto. It should, for example, encourage investment in labor-intensive industries—and insist that it go to businesses whose black workers enjoy the protection of the Sullivan principles. In a country where only 2,000 of the estimated 70,000 black teachers have a high school education, the United States should also assist the development of a multinational teaching corps.

In short, the United States should try a policy of enlightened engagement with South Africa. Sending Michael Jackson to Soweto would be a provocative first step—and that would only be the beginning. We need to show the blacks of South Africa that we care about their plight, and to remind the whites that we are watching.

Reverend Leon H. Sullivan is the pastor of Zion Baptist Church in Philadelphia and the author of the Sullivan Principles, a code of ethics for US businessmen in South Africa. He is also the founder of the Opportunities Industrialization Centers of America. William J. Choyke, a reporter for The Dallas Morning News, *spent 10 days in 1984 in South Africa.*

"I believe it is time for U.S. corporations to get out—all the way out, and as fast as they can."

US Corporations Cannot Change South Africa

Clifton R. Wharton Jr.

Many thoughtful Americans, deeply sympathetic to the oppressed black majority in South Africa, have believed or wanted to believe that U.S. business interests in that nation could blunt the cruelty of systematic apartheid. For some years, and with much uneasiness, I took the same position.

Now I believe it is time for U.S. corporations to get out—all the way out, and as fast as they can.

As an American black, I have always found the concept of apartheid abhorrent. One of the most degrading and dehumanizing practices ever institutionalized in a supposedly civilized country, it rivals in many respects the genocidal programs of Adolf Hitler. Pervasive, crushing, unspeakable— apartheid never has been and never can be anything more than a mortal affront to freedom and human dignity.

But what could we in America do to confront the atrocity? As an academic, I had to believe that brutality would eventually give way under the overwhelming moral weight of humane education. As an American citizen, I hoped that the weight of U.S. foreign policy would more squarely support world opinion, convincing even an obdurate Pretoria to abandon its fanaticism.

And as a corporate director, I hoped that enlightened, nondiscriminating, U.S.-style management at American plants in South Africa would provide economic opportunities for some blacks, while setting a progressive example for the country as a whole.

A majority of U.S. firms had adopted the so-called Sullivan principles, mandating equal treatment, pay and opportunity for their nonwhite South African employees. Numerous black leaders there as well as in the United States offered their reluctant

Clifton R. Wharton Jr., "U.S. Business Has No Place in South Africa," *Minneapolis Star and Tribune*, March 25, 1985. Originally published in *Newsday*. Reprinted with the author's permission.

endorsement, while continuing to denounce and oppose any settlement or cease-fire with apartheid itself.

South Africa Is a Pariah

But if this position was ever tenable, it is no longer. In commerce and foreign policy alike, we must treat the South African government as the pariah it long ago chose to become.

What has altered my view? A slow but inexorable tilt in the balance of outrage, as the damning evidence continued to mount.

In 1981, the Rockefeller Foundation supported a commission chaired by Franklin Thomas, president of the foundation. The group's exhaustive study of South African apartheid led to a report titled "Time Running Out." It spelled out in detail the scores of elaborate, ingenious and malevolent mechanisms by which a small white minority separates peoples, creates phantom "homelands" and administers the legalized enslavement of 22 million blacks.

I took part in a meeting convened by Thomas to determine what changes, if any, have occurred since publication of his report. True, it is clear that U.S. corporations have had some positive impact on the lives of the 66,000 South African blacks the Sullivan-principle firms employ. But for the millions not lucky enough to work for U.S. firms, conditions are worse than ever.

Conditions Worse for Blacks

Far from any generalized liberalization having resulted from the presence of American companies, the great majority of black South Africans have seen their economic well-being and human rights actually eroded during the last three years.

An April 1984 conference in Johannesburg heard some 300 papers resulting from the Carnegie Foundation study of poverty in South Africa. In the aggregate, they documented a significant increase in the impoverishment of blacks. A study by Charles Simkins of Capetown University, for example, found that the number of homeland people living below a "minimum living level" standard increased from 4.9 million to 8.9 million between 1960 and 1980.

What will happen if U.S. firms withdraw entirely from commercial activity in South Africa? Some have argued that their presence has until now had a moderating influence on behalf of evolutionary reform, while abrupt withdrawal is criticized as likely to touch off a revolutionary explosion.

Realism suggests that the drama of corporate withdrawal may not, in itself, have a proportionately forceful effect on apartheid. Non-U.S. firms may well move in to take up the slack, even in the face of world censure. But that does not mean that getting U.S. corporations out of South Africa would be self-defeating.

Corporate Conscience

Corporate conscience is an elusive idea in this country, but it exists and cries out to be heeded. When the eventual explosion comes in South Africa, it is our conscience, no less that of world opinion, that will call us to account. If our firms are still there, how will we explain and justify our tacit collusion with evil?

In the meantime, a U.S. commercial disengagement would certainly cause economic hardships for South Africa. It would further inflict Pretoria in the eyes of the world, and it would place greater stigma on any nations and companies moving in to replace the departed Americans.

"When a human situation so fundamentally affronts every tenet of human values, a public expression of personal opposition is a moral obligation."

What about the few black South Africans who have made tangible gains through employment by U.S. firms? Tragically, they will suffer.

My conviction on withdrawal is strengthened by the position of Bishop Desmond Tutu, the newest recipient of the Nobel peace prize, who was elected the first black Anglican bishop of Johannesburg. Noting that U.S. corporations have prospered from doing business in South Africa, Tutu has admonished that their role should not be to make apartheid "more comfortable.". . .

Are advocates of divestiture really prepared to boycott or forgo every consumer product that uses South African chrome? Better yet, will they boycott the New York gold and diamond firms whose wares

are far more massively and directly linked to black semi-slave labor in South African mines?

Aside from their brief publicity value, divestiture campaigns inflict no "punishment" on South Africa. While divestiture might salve the egos of those activists who are indiscriminately against "big business," it would have no direct effect on the real matters at hand. All that would happen is that somebody else would buy the stock.

For that matter, even a total U.S. corporate withdrawal is unlikely to be enough of an American response.

Foreign Policy Best Weapon

I believe that national foreign policy is the strongest and most effective weapon in our arsenal against apartheid. The United States should have a unilateral policy of total economic sanctions against Pretoria, and we should cooperate with the United Nations to encourage complete economic, social and cultural isolation.

Unhappily, the present administration's policy of "constructive engagement" with South Africa is not only a delusion and a sham; it actively undercuts the cause of the black majority and those other groups who are also systematically oppressed there. By giving only the weakest lip service to opposing the harsh debasement of human rights, President Ronald Reagan has signaled that minority tyranny need fear no reprisals that present any true threat to apartheid or the economic and political status quo.

Does the administration's indifference stem from a vain hope that the problem will go away? Does it have to do with the chromium, platinum, ferromanganese and vanadium that South Africa provides to our stockpile of strategic materials?

Certainly strategic metals are important to our national security. But is there no way to acquire them save through a Faustian pact that barters away the souls of millions of human beings?

Finally, there comes a point so incompatible with one's respect for humanity itself that compromises with conscience can no longer be tolerated or rationalized. When a human situation so fundamentally affronts every tenet of human values, a public expression of personal opposition is a moral obligation.

But individual protests are no substitute for political will. There is no better way, and no other way, to reassert our national integrity than to act decisively, and to act now. For U.S. corporations in South Africa, time has run out.

Clifton R. Wharton Jr., a chancellor of the State University of New York, is chairman of the board of the Rockefeller Foundation and a director of the Ford Motor Company.

"This covert enterprise...will not bring the Sandinistas to President Reagan's feet, and it will not overthrow them. It will confirm and not undermine their Marxist-Leninist leanings."

The US Should Not Aid the Contras

McGeorge Bundy

The dismal historical record of covert military and paramilitary operations over the last 25 years is entirely clear. We even know some of the reasons for that record.

Characteristically, the exiles who are willing to accept money and direction from the CIA are not as a group the most dedicated democrats from their own society. Characteristically, agency recruiters prefer military professionals to enthusiastic amateurs, but such military professionals, especially the graduates of repressive authoritarian armies, do not ordinarily have great skill in guerrilla operations. Characteristically, agency officials under pressure for results are driven to increasingly harebrained schemes, and not all of them are honestly and fully explained to superiors or to authorized committees of Congress.

Characteristically, moreover, revolutionary governments under this kind of attack give the highest possible priority to defeating it. The very existence of the antigovernmental forces becomes a powerful incentive to increased militarization, increased domestic repression, and the dedication of a nation in arms to the destruction of the intruders. And with regret I must add that in the Caribbean area, where fear and suspicion of the Yankee colossus have deep historical roots, the knowledge that an operation is bought and paid for by the CIA becomes a most powerful reinforcement of the very government whose overthrow is sought.

I begin by emphasizing the ineffectiveness of covert action for the overthrow of a government because I am persuaded that it is precisely the overthrow of the Nicaraguan government—the replacement of the present Sandinista leadership, by one means or another—that is the fundamental objective of the administration.

For a long time the announced purpose of the covert program was to inhibit or prevent Nicaraguan assistance to the insurgents in El Salvador. I did not find it easy to be confident that this asserted purpose was all that the administration had in mind, but I believed that there was a certain rough justice in its asserted objective, and even some hope that an operation with this limited purpose might have some success, either in making any Nicaraguan export of revolution harder, or in leading to some form of live-and-let-live agreement.

The Real Purpose

But now the president has made it clear that his real purpose is very much larger, nothing less than the transformation of the government of Nicaragua, and it therefore becomes necessary to say as forcefully as possible that covert action cannot by itself produce this result. If the president will ask the estimators at the CIA for their own best judgment on this point, I am confident that this is what they will tell him.

The judgment I have given you is entirely independent of any certain conclusion, one way or the other, on the question whether the current Nicaraguan regime is or is not irrevocably committed to the establishment of a totalitarian Marxist-Leninist regime with an active engagement in the export of violent revolution. I do not know how to make a firm prediction on that important question. What I do know is that covert action, without more, makes the worst result more and not less likely. The very existence of the CIA-backed contras plays into the hands of the hardest of the hard-liners in a government about which we have good reason to be wary....

Given the current attitude of the administration and the choices it wishes to force upon the Nicaraguan government, it is totally predictable that

McGeorge Bundy, "Covert Operations Like This One Are Doomed to Failure," *The Washington Times*, April 22, 1985. Reprinted with permission.

the delay proposed by the president will have no fruitful result and that he will then put the money into military support.

Lessons from History

So the real question. . .is whether or not to put more money into covert military operations. On that question I find the negative judgment of history conclusive.

There is one other lesson from history. Over the years supporters of covert action have won approval for their proposals, as far as they have, by appealing to the double belief of an administration, first, that it must do *something,* and second, that it has nothing else to do. This was the mode in which successive American administrations approached Cuba in earlier years, and as I read the record of the debates of recent years here in Congress, I find the same theme constantly reiterated by the administration's supporters: we don't like covert operations, and we know their effectiveness is doubtful, but we certainly have to do something about this Marxist-Leninist cat's-paw of the Soviet Union and Cuba. It is indeed a hallmark of covert operations that they are the consequence of a belief that no better instrument is available. I believe that this way of thinking is deeply wrong and arises from too timid an estimate of what can be justified when a good case is made.

Other Options

Let us consider the two basic possibilities that lie ahead for the present Nicaraguan government.

It may well be that this government, if it remains in power, will inexorably persist in an increasingly Marxist-Leninist course, with increasing reliance on Soviet and Cuban assistance, and an increasing commitment to the export of violent revolution. I do not know that this will be the result, but I do know that if that is the chosen course, the United States will indeed have a deep national interest in taking fully effective means to reverse it.

In my view, the nature of the most effective means has been defined, for the Caribbean area, by our experience in the Cuban missile crisis.

It is our control of the seas that can defeat and reverse any such Nicaraguan choice. What we would require for the use of our sea power is regional support, and regional support in turn would require a clarity of our own exposition and concreteness in our own purposes, which, to put it mildly, we have not yet had from this administration. When President Reagan seeks to frighten Americans with the specter of 100 million enslaved by Moscow, and refugees assaulting our borders by the tens of millions, he is describing a situation which certainly cannot be prevented by the naval forces responsive to the president as commander-in-chief.

Now let us consider the other possibility: that there is no inevitability in the future course of the Nicaraguan government, that it can become open to pluralism in its own country and respectful of the rights of its neighbors, that it can become a party to a live-and-let-live arrangement, and that it can recognize its own deep interest in staying away from the slippery slope of increasing dependence on Havana and Moscow.

Let us suppose also that the neighbors of Nicaragua, both within the region and within the wider Contadora group, and indeed in Latin America as a whole, can decide to exert their own substantial influence in this general direction. Is there not advantage in leaving this road open, rather than building roadblocks across it by implacable insistence on covert war?

Doomed to Failure

I do not have a crystal ball that can tell me which way the Sandinista government will move. We must be prepared to make continuing judgments on its course, and we will be helped and not hindered if in that process we make a much more serious use of diplomacy than we have chosen so far. Meanwhile, we can improve the chance of a good result, and increase our own and our neighbors' understanding of what will be necessary in the event of a bad one, if the Congress has the will and the courage to maintain its current and entirely reasonable judgment that loosening of the purse strings for covert war would be a serious self-inflicted wound to our national interest.

"Characteristically, the exiles who are willing to accept money and direction from the CIA are not as a group the most dedicated democrats from their own society."

Let me in closing simply underline my basic point. This covert enterprise, by itself, is doomed to failure. It will not bring the Sandinistas to President Reagan's feet, and it will not overthrow them. It will confirm and not undermine their Marxist-Leninist leanings. It will not fulfill the hopes of the democrats among the contras, or the ambitions of their somocista officers. It will shed blood on all sides, and it will intensify the existing polarization among Nicaraguans. It will bring discredit on our government among millions of our own citizens and more millions of friends abroad. It will make constructive change in Nicaragua less likely, and regional support for any necessary, stronger course much harder to obtain. So it will do great harm along the way, and *it simply will not work.*

McGeorge Bundy was a presidential advisor to former Presidents Kennedy and Johnson and currently teaches history at New York University.

"[If the US stops aiding the contras] the Soviets and the Cubans could...do what they do best—making revolution— while the guilt-ridden West also does what it does best—paying for it."

viewpoint 120

The US Should Aid the Contras

Mark Falcoff

At this point, the Nicaraguan controversy in the United States has gone beyond debate over who is responsible for the present situation to the propriety or convenience of supporting—at first covertly, then semi-covertly, and perhaps eventually openly—the Nicaraguan counterrevolutionaries, or contras....

Some objections to this policy are wholly legalistic: critics point to the U.S. Neutrality Act and long-standing commitments under various OAS treaties not to intervene in the affairs of member states. If the aim of foreign policy is for the United States to demonstrate its adherence to the rule of law above all other considerations, including the right to counter the illegal activities of other parties, then such prohibition should be observed literally and aid to the contras should be immediately terminated. But this should be done in the clear prospect of no other favorable outcome than, at best, a momentary public-relations victory: the United States might claim some position of virtue in debate at international forums, and the Sandinistas would have to find new ways of blaming Washington for all that ails their country. Neither of these satisfactions is likely to alter the situation on the ground, where on the contrary a cutoff of aid to the insurgents would enable the Sandinistas further to consolidate their hold on power at home and would free them for more extensive activities elsewhere.

A second objection to the policy of aiding the contras is that it purportedly places the United States in league with the darkest elements of the Nicaraguan past, the old National Guard, which served for decades as the watchdog (and bully-boy) of the Somoza dynasty. These are men whom Speaker Thomas P. O'Neill has colorfully labeled "murderers, marauders, and rapists."

Mark Falcoff, "How to Understand Central America." Reprinted from *Commentary*, September 1984, by permission; all rights reserved.

Actually, there are three different contra forces— the FDN (Nicaraguan Democratic Force), the ARDE (Democratic Revolutionary Action), and the FARN (Nicaraguan Armed Revolutionary Forces). The FDN comes closest to justifying Speaker O'Neill's remark, since it is officered by former Guardsmen and commanded by former Guard General Enrique Bermudez. Even so, as Richard Millett, a veteran student (and critic) of the Nicaraguan military, has pointed out in the Carnegie study, Bermudez does not fully fit the *somocista* mold. He was "viewed by Somoza as too popular with the troops and not sufficiently committed to the Somoza family," Millett writes, and during the last years of the dictatorship he was consigned to virtual "diplomatic exile" in the United States and Japan. Consequently, he had no connection with the atrocities associated with Somoza's final years of power.

The "Democratic Left"

The ARDE, on the other hand, is led by Eden Pastora, and officered not by ex-Guardsmen but by ex-Sandinistas. In fact, these people are the "democratic Left" the United States is always being urged to support in Latin America; in this particular incarnation, however, such democratic leftism provokes discomfort and aversion in its North American counterpart. Ironically, far from being puppets of the CIA, Pastora and his men have pointedly distanced themselves from it, and are reliably reported to be distrusted by the Reagan administration. As for the tiny FARN, it is of minor importance; though its leader Fernando Chamorro and his lieutenants are undoubtedly conservative, they have no ties to the Somoza dynasty or the old National Guard.

This is certainly a more complex picture than Speaker O'Neill has painted; and when one examines the base of these movements, the picture becomes more complex still. FDN draws its fighting force—in some estimates as much as 10,000 men—from peasants, small landowners, and shopkeepers who resent the Sandinistas for religious or ideological reasons. Many, Millett reports, are Miskito Indians "reacting to Sandinista actions which have disrupted their traditional pattern of living, destroyed their homes, and transformed them into bitter refugees." ARDE's small army—about 2,000 combatants—is also an amalgam of Miskito Indians, veterans of the 1978-79 civil war against Somoza, and civilians active in the struggle against the old dictatorship, notably Alfonso Robelo.

"At the level of the rank-and-file the contras are not fighting and dying to enthrone a new Somoza, or even to obtain veterans' pensions from the CIA."

Clearly, whatever differences may exist at the top, at the level of the rank-and-file the contras are not fighting and dying to enthrone a new Somoza, or even to obtain veterans' pensions from the CIA (as if such things existed). While the work of the FDN would be more difficult without "covert" U.S. aid, the example of ARDE strongly suggests that for the Sandinstas this is a problem which even in the absence of U.S. involvement will not go away.

Contra Goals

Finally, it is often said that the contras are not really fighting, as they claim, to compel the Sandinistas to live up to their promises to the OAS, or (as the U.S. government additionally claims) to interrupt arms traffic to neighboring countries, but are rather attempting to overthrow the Nicaraguan government. When and if this happens, it is added, the differences between the FDN and the ARDE will make the country ungovernable. Oddly enough, this view is advanced by people who only yesterday saw nothing improbable in an alliance between Sandinistas and Nicaraguan democrats, and who today are likely to commend a coalition government in El Salvador between the Christian Democrats and the FMLN.

As it happens, however, the contras have repeatedly stated that they will lay down their arms if and when the Sandinistas permit genuinely free elections and open the political process so that all elements of the opposition may freely organize and campaign. . . . The Sandinistas need not even believe in the contras' sincerity to test their offer: were they to do what the contras have asked, there would be no possibility of the Reagan administration's successfully reviving in Congress the aid program to the FDN, and the contras themselves would suffer massive defections from their ranks. It is entirely possible that even now the Sandinistas would win such elections, but in a subsequent political order in which the opposition had a legitimate role they would have to accept some of the restraints characteristic of pluralistic political systems. This is admittedly an unlikely outcome, but less likely still in the absence of the kinds of pressures which the contras are uniquely positioned to apply. . . .

Thinly-Disguised Defeat

Most critics of present U.S. policy in Central America advocate some kind of multilateral diplomatic solution, in which the Contadora countries, the United States, and, in some scenarios, Spain, France, and Cuba would negotiate a regional settlement. Given the diversity of interests which would have to be harmonized, it is difficult to imagine what that agreement would look like, much less who would enforce it—unless one imagines that all nations are created equal in power and influence, that ideology counts for nothing in international relations, and that all treaties are self-enforcing. Some people do in fact believe all these things, and during the Carter administration they proved it by ultimately consigning the fate of Nicaragua to the Organization of American States. Just why that method should work now when it did not work under far more auspicious circumstances five years ago is a deep mystery. But perhaps what is really being proposed is the withdrawal of the United States from the Caribbean Basin and a thinly-disguised military and diplomatic defeat in our oldest area of security concern.

No doubt many of the same people would sincerely regret such an outcome. They advocate a "multilateral" way out of the Central American labyrinth only because they believe . . . that our present course will inevitably lead to "what almost everyone still opposes, deployment of U.S. combat troops in Central America." This is an argument which on its very face is supposed to silence objections to the various utopian proposals making the rounds of the study commissions, congressional committees, and op-ed pages.

It is not an argument to be taken lightly, but given the current environment of public opinion in the United States, combined with the institutional restraints now imposed by the War Powers Act, there is not much change that troops will actually be deployed. . . .

Paying for Soviet Revolutions

Having nearly foreclosed the option of covert action, are we to discard as well not merely the use of military force but even its threat? In that case, the task of U.S. diplomacy, at least in the Third World, would be limited to disbursing largesse—in large quantities to friends, but also in large quantities to adversaries, in the hope of "influencing" them favorably. If even that failed to produce the desirable outcome, the United States could still be blamed (or could still blame itself) for not giving enough aid, for not giving it rapidly enough, or for attaching too many conditions to it. Meanwhile, the Soviets and the Cubans could reap the benefits of a new international division of labor, in which they would do what they do best—making revolution—while the guilt-ridden West also does what it does best—paying for it. This is a recipe not merely for failure but for suicide.

Over the last four years a curious cloud of historicism has settled over discussion of Central America, as if the world were created around 1965 and Vietnam were our only experience of situations of this kind. In his recent book *The Real Peace*, Richard Nixon recalls that in 1947, when President Truman was attempting to resist the Communist seizure of power in Greece, Congress was flooded with an orchestrated campaign of correspondence demanding that "food, not arms" be delivered to the beleaguered government of that country. Had Congress taken that advice, the outcome in Greece would have been very different—and not merely for the monarchy (which has since disappeared), the military (which has been returned to the barracks), or the wealthy (now subjected to new taxes). Without the action taken by Truman, it is simply inconceivable that Greece would have a democratic government today, much less one which is both socialist and independent of the Soviet Union. . . .

"Given the diversity of interests which would have to be harmonized, it is difficult to imagine what [a multilateral diplomatic] agreement would look like, much less who would enforce it."

The Central American labyrinth has its own, unique ground plan. We may not find our way out easily or quickly, or even under terms which fully satisfy us, much less our Central American neighbors. But we should be clear about what we are seeking, what outcomes are most probable, and what their human, political, and strategic costs will be. There is no shortcut; those who suggest that there is one are deceiving us, and probably themselves as well.

Mark Falcoff is a resident fellow at the American Enterprise Institute and has recently written Crisis and Opportunity: U.S. Policy in the Caribbean and Central America *with Robert Royal.*

"The idea of publicly backing 'freedom fighters' around the world has been elevated to a basic principle of foreign policy by President Reagan."

viewpoint**121**

The Reagan Doctrine: An Overview

Doyle McManus

The Reagan Administration is developing a sweeping new foreign policy doctrine that provides for a more assertive U.S. role in the Third World. From Nicaragua to Angola, from Afghanistan to Cambodia, Administration officials say, the United States should actively—and overtly—back rebellions against pro-Soviet regimes.

Born in the congressional fight over aid to the anti-Sandinista rebels in Nicaragua, the idea of publicly backing "freedom fighters" around the world has been elevated to a basic principle of foreign policy by President Reagan.

Hawks in the Administration, allied with hard-liners in Congress and conservative lobbying groups outside the government, are working to promote a steadily wider application of what some call the "Reagan Doctrine."

"We must not break faith with those who are risking their lives—on every continent, from Afghanistan to Nicaragua—to defy Soviet-supported aggression and secure rights which have been ours since birth," Reagan declared in his State of the Union Address [in 1985]. "Support for freedom fighters is self-defense."

Assistant Secretary of Defense Richard L. Armitage, one of the architects of the new doctrine, said: "If a group is fighting a repressive regime and shares our values and our goals, then we have very little choice but to support them. For us, the issue is not whether freedom fighters deserve our support; the real question is what support should be offered."

Fundamental Questions

There is also a continuing question within the Administration and among its outside supporters over exactly how a policy of support for anti-communist rebels should be carried out. At issue are such points as how much aid should be sent, to whom and how openly.

Senate conservatives, for example, advocate a major increase in overt aid for a wide range of insurgent movements. State and Defense Department officials, by contrast, tend to argue for more covert aid, and more caution.

"We're still working on a doctrine on this," a senior State Department official said. "I don't think anybody had thought about it in global terms before. . . . It's all been on a case-by-case basis."

As the new doctrine gains public visibility, officials acknowledge that they will have to answer some fundamental questions. Among them:

—Should the United States adopt the Soviet strategy of promoting revolutions against governments it dislikes?

—How should the President choose which regimes to destabilize and which to leave alone?

—Will U.S. support for insurgencies hinder or encourage peaceful solutions?

Nonetheless, although the details are subject to debate, the Administration has clearly settled on the basic theme of a new policy toward Third World conflicts. The United States has a right and a duty to help rebels who take up arms against Marxist regimes—and an opportunity to help topple some governments.

Heartening Examples

"After years of guerrilla insurgencies led by Communists against pro-Western governments, we now see dramatic and heartening examples of popular insurgencies against Communist regimes," Secretary of State George P. Shultz told the senate Foreign Relations Committee. "If we turned our backs. . .we would be conceding the Soviet notion that Communist revolutions are irreversible while everything else is up for grabs."

Doyle McManus, "U.S. Shaping Assertive Policy for Third World," *Los Angeles Times*, June 16, 1985. © 1985, Los Angeles Times Syndicate. Reprinted with permission.

Said a Defense Department official: "We're talking about getting involved in insurgency now—rather than what we did in the '60s, which was mainly counterinsurgency. Socialism is not irreversible.... We do not rule out playing by the same kind of rules the Soviets do. Up until now, we haven't been playing on a level field. We'd like to even it out a little bit."

In the past, U.S. involvement in uprisings has been limited in scope and, normally, as clandestine as the CIA could make it. The United States supported an abortive insurgency in Albania in 1949, successful coups in Iran and Guatemala in 1954, the Bay of Pigs invasion of Cuba in 1961 and the opposition to Chile's Marxist government in 1973. Those actions were neither publicly announced nor raised to the level of a general "doctrine."

Moral Duty

Today, however, Reagan Administration spokesmen say that the rash of new pro-Soviet regimes that came to power after the fall of South Vietnam in 1975—in Cambodia, Angola, Mozambique, Ethiopia, Nicaragua and Afghanistan—prompted spontaneous rebellions from their citizens, and that the United States has a moral duty to lend them at least political support.

Borrowing a phrase once used by Americans who complained that the U.S. government too often supported repressive regimes abroad, proponents of the Reagan Doctrine contend that it is putting this country "on the side of history."

The basic premises of the new Reagan Doctrine have drawn little criticism from Democrats in Congress. Some have fought the President on aid to rebels in Nicaragua, but some, like liberal Rep. Stephen J. Solarz (D-N.Y.), have actually led the drive for more overt aid to insurgents in Afghanistan and Cambodia.

Administration officials suggest that Solarz "does that so he can attack us on Nicaragua without looking soft on communism."

Solarz waves away that suggestion, saying: "In the debate between internationalism and isolationism, I definitely come down on the side of internationalism. We should not try to be the world's policeman, but we can't afford to be a naive bystander watching with indifference while the Soviet Union and its surrogates subvert countries."

Interventionism Feared

A few voices on Capitol Hill still inveigh against intervention in the Third World in tones reminiscent of the Vietnam War era.

"We're doing things just because the Soviets and their surrogates are doing them, and that puts us in the same gutter with them," said Rep. Jim Leach (R-Iowa), a moderate GOP maverick. "Where has American intervention ever helped in the Third World? I'd rather play on our field, by our rules."

Leach acknowledged, though that the tide is running against him.... The Democratic-led House voted solidly to renew U.S. funding for the Nicaraguan rebels known as *contras*, reversing two years of opposition to the once-covert program. And the Senate voted to repeal the 1975 prohibition on aid to Angolan rebels, a measure that had been a landmark of anti-interventionist sentiment after Vietnam; the House has yet to act on the issue.

The new doctrine of aiding anti-communist rebels, proponents say, is a logical outgrowth of the developments of the last decade. After the fall of Vietnam, pro-Soviet regimes came to power in Angola, Mozambique, Ethiopia and Nicaragua; Communist Vietnam invaded neighboring Communist Cambodia; and, in 1979, the Soviet Union itself invaded Afghanistan.

In all those countries, Administration officials say, the new pro-Soviet regimes proved to be belligerent and repressive, and pro-Western insurgencies formed to fight them.

Political Climate

An equally important factor may be the return of both the Democratic and Republican parties to the moralistic tradition of American foreign policy—the Democrats in the human rights crusade of Jimmy Carter, the GOP in the anti-communism of Ronald Reagan.

"The United States today is not the United States of a decade ago, one that was full of self-doubts," the Pentagon's Armitage said. "We're a different nation now. We're a very confident nation. Under Ronald Reagan, we're a stronger nation. We aren't afraid to stand up for what we believe in, and that includes human rights.... Under Communist regimes, human rights are not highly regarded."

"Debate continues over how many insurgencies the United States should sponsor."

The political climate may have turned friendly to the kind of indirect intervention the Reagan Administration endorses, but debate continues over how many insurgencies the United States should sponsor, what kind of aid it should give and whether the U.S. role should be covert or publicly declared.

Patchwork of Positions

In a series of case-by-case decisions in the past, the Administration has come to adopt a patchwork of positions that senior officials concede is inconsistent:

—In Afghanistan, it secretly sent more than $380 million in military aid to the anti-Soviet rebels before pressure from Senate conservatives prompted it to acknowledge openly that it has supplied small amounts of "humanitarian aid" as well.

—In Nicaragua, the Administration began by secretly sending the contras more than $80 million in military aid, as well as CIA commando teams but found itself forced to go public with support for the contras after Congress—angry over a covert effort to mine Nicaragua's harbors—cut the rebels off.

—In Cambodia, the Administration wanted to aid anti-communist rebels indirectly, through other Southeast Asian countries, but Solarz and others in Congress are insisting on at least a symbolic $5 million in direct, overt U.S. aid.

"The Administration's conservative allies—and prodders—are creating a new factor on Capitol Hill: a rebel lobby."

Conversely, in Angola, the Administration has been barred by law from helping pro-Western rebels, but officials say they have made no decision on whether they would want to do this. And in Ethiopia and Mozambique, the Administration has looked at anti-Soviet guerrilla movements and decided that they do not deserve U.S. support.

Rebel Lobbyists

Conservatives such as Sens. Steven D. Symms (R-Idaho), Robert Kasten (R-Wis.) and Malcolm Wallop (R-Wyo.), backed by a growing number of would-be rebel lobbyists, want the Administration to increase its aid to insurgents, especially the Angolans and Mozambicans.

Kasten, chairman of the Senate Appropriations subcommittee on foreign operations, is considering a proposal to give the President an unrestricted $50-million "rebel fund" for the insurgents of his choice.

The conservatives charge that the State Department has been resisting any expansion of rebel aid, despite Shultz's frequent speeches on the subject. Some even say that the CIA has been insufficiently enthusiastic about the Afghan rebels. Wallop has proposed a new White House "office for freedom fighters" to take charge of promoting insurgents' causes.

"The bureaucracy doesn't always work the way it should," Symms said. "Our overwhelming urge to be diplomats sometimes overcomes our ability to lay down the gauntlet."

Framework for Support

On the other side of the issue, Democrat Solarz has contended that the Administration should finance rebel movements only in countries under foreign invasion—a test that would allow aid to the Afghans and Cambodians but not the Nicaraguans, Angolans or Mozambicans.

"We need to make these decisions in a conceptual framework that will not lead to us getting involved in all kinds of conflicts that may not be in our national interest," Solarz said. "There are those who think the only criterion should be whether the rebels oppose the Communists. . . . That seems to me to be a formula for widespread interventionism."

Solarz said he opposes aid to the Nicaraguan contras, for example, because "we would be supporting an effort to overthrow an internationally recognized government."

Within the Administration, the debate is narrower. Officials say that Defense Secretary Caspar W. Weinberger and the Pentagon are enthusiastic about expanded aid to rebels, while Shultz's State Department is more cautious. Defense Department officials have supported overt aid, but Shultz and National Security Adviser Robert C. McFarlane are said to prefer covert aid.

"Covert action is carried out for the most part in cooperation with somebody else—some friendly government that is often weak, anxious and fearful of the cost of open dependence on us," Donald R. Fortier, a McFarlane aide, said. "We have to be sensitive to (our allies') weaknesses and vulnerabilities."

Prodding the Administration

Meanwhile, the Administration's conservative allies—and prodders—are creating a new factor on Capitol Hill: a rebel lobby.

Jeane J. Kirkpatrick, former ambassador to the United Nations, and former Treasury Secretary William E. Simon are making speeches and raising money for the Nicaraguan contras. Moser and an assortment of other anti-communist activists have formed the Resistance Support Alliance.

And Lewis Lehrman—a millionaire conservative activist who airlifted Nicaraguan, Afghan and Laotian opposition figures into the Angolan bush . . . for a first-ever convention of "freedom fighters"—has undertaken a new project: a professionally staffed Washington lobbying office for the rebels.

"These guys haven't really been able to articulate to Congress how they should be helped," said Jack Abramoff, a former Republican National Committee staff member and Lehrman aide. "We hope to give them some help on that. We see this as a contribution to the overall Reagan Doctrine. Every time we've worked with anybody in the Administration, we've gotten nothing but help. . . . It's a trend, and we're on the move."

Doyle McManus is a staff writer for the Los Angeles Times.

"If a revolution is both popular and democratic, it is hard to see the moral objection to extending it support."

The Reagan Doctrine Is Sound

Charles Krauthammer

Ronald Reagan is the master of the new idea, and has built the most successful political career in a half-century launching one after another. His list of credits includes small government (Barry Goldwater having tried, and failed, with it first), supply-side economics and strategic defense (Star Wars). These radically changed the terms of debate on the welfare state, economic theory and nuclear strategy. All that was left for him to turn on its head was accepted thinking on geopolitics. Now he has done that too. He has produced the Reagan Doctrine. . . .

American Tradition

The Reagan Doctrine proclaims overt and unashamed American support for anti-Communist revolution. The grounds are justice, necessity and democratic tradition. Justice, said the President. . .because these revolutionaries are "fighting for an end to tyranny." Necessity, said Secretary of State George Shultz. . .because if these "freedom fighters" are defeated, their countries will be irrevocably lost behind an Iron Curtain of Soviet domination. And democratic tradition, said the President, because to support "our brothers" in revolution is to continue—"in Afghanistan, in Ethiopia, Cambodia, Angola. . .[and] Nicaragua"—200 years of American support for "Simon Bolivar. . .the Polish patriots, the French Resistance and others seeking freedom."

That tradition ended abruptly with Viet Nam. It is true that President Carter sent arms to the Afghan rebels and that Congress concurred. Congress has also gone along with economic aid to the non-Communist resistance in Cambodia. However, since the Clark Amendment of 1976 prohibiting aid to anti-Marxist fighters in Angola, Congress has refused to support war against indigenous Communist

dictatorships, no matter how heavily supported by the Soviet Union or its proxies. President Reagan's program of CIA support for the Nicaraguan *contras*, who are not fighting foreign occupation, broke post-Viet Nam precedent. At first, and for three long years, that new policy was given the flimsiest of justifications: interdicting supplies to the Salvadoran guerrillas. The Reagan Doctrine drops the fig leaf. It is intended to establish a new, firmer—a doctrinal—foundation for such support by declaring equally worthy all armed resistance to Communism, whether foreign or indigenously imposed.

To interpret the Reagan Doctrine as merely a puffed-up rationale for Nicaraguan policy is like calling the Truman Doctrine a cover for a new Greek and Turkish policy. In both cases, the principles established have a much more profound implication.

The Truman Doctrine set out the basic foreign policy axiom of the postwar era: containment. With J.F.K.'s pledge to "bear any burden. . .to assure. . .the success of liberty," the idea of containment reached its most expansive and consensually accepted stage. With Viet Nam, the consensus and the expansiveness collapsed. Since then the U.S. has oscillated, at times erratically, between different approaches—different doctrines—for defending its ideals and its interests.

The Reagan Doctrine is the third such attempt since Viet Nam. The first was the Nixon Doctrine: relying on friendly regimes to police their regions. Unfortunately, the jewel in the crown of this theory was the Shah of Iran. Like him, it was retired in 1979 to a small Panamanian island. Next came the Carter Doctrine, declaring a return to unilateral American action, if necessary, in defense of Western interests. That doctrine rests on the emergency of a rapid deployment force. Unfortunately, the force turned out neither rapid nor deployable. It enjoys a vigorous theoretical existence in southern Florida, whence it is poorly situated to repel the Red Army.

Rolling Back Communism

If regional powers prove unstable, and projected American power unreliable, what then? It is a precious irony that the answer to that question has been suggested to Americans by a band of fanatical Islamic warriors in Afghanistan. Unaware of their historic contribution to the theory of containment, they took on the Soviet army, made it bleed and slowed its march to the more coveted goal, the warm waters of the Persian Gulf.

This insurgency, and those in Cambodia, Angola and Nicaragua, pointed to a new form of containment, a kind of ex post facto containment: harassment of Soviet expansionism at the limits of empire. There is an echo here of the old 1950s right-wing idea of "rolling back" Communism. But with a difference. This is not the reckless—and toothless—call for reclaiming the core Soviet possessions in Eastern Europe, which the Soviets claim for self-defense and, more important, which they are prepared to use the most extreme means to retain. This is a challenge to the peripheral acquisitions of empire.

The Brezhnev Doctrine proclaimed in 1968 that the Soviet sphere only expands. The Reagan Doctrine is meant as its antithesis. It declares that the U.S. will work at the periphery to reverse that expansion. How? Like the Nixon Doctrine, it turns to proxies. Unlike the Nixon Doctrine, it supports not the status quo but revolution.

"The grounds [for the Reagan Doctrine] are justice, necessity and democratic tradition."

And that makes it so hard for both left and right to digest. For the left it seems all quite paradoxical, and hypocritical: the Administration denounces Salvadoran guerrillas for blowing up power stations and attacking villages, while at the same time it supports Nicaraguan guerrillas who are doing the same thing only a few miles away. But the idea that intellectual honesty requires one to be for or against all revolution is absurd. You judge a revolution, as you do any other political phenomenon, by what it stands for. Suppose you believe that justice was on the side of the central government in the American Civil War. Does that commit you to oppose the Paris Commune of 1870 or the Hungarian revolution of 1956? In Salvador, the rebels want to overthrow the President, a Christian Democrat. In Nicaragua, the rebels want to overthrow the President, a Marxist-Leninist. To judge rebels by who they are and what they fight for, and against, is not a political morality of convenience. It is simple logic.

Supporting Revolution

On the right, the idea of supporting revolution is equally hard to accept, though for different reasons. Conservatives may find it easier to support revolution in practice than in theory. This is already obvious from their choice of words. Reagan finds it hard to call the good guys rebels. Instead, he insists on calling them "freedom fighters," a heavy, inconvenient term, with an unmistakable socialist-realist ring. "Freedom fighters" practically announces itself as a term of bias. Rebels, Mr. President. With practice, it will get easier to say.

Language, however, is the easier problem facing the Reagan Doctrine. Morality poses thornier ones. By what right does the U.S. take sides in foreign civil wars? What about sovereignty? What about international law?

The President may be revolutionary, but he is not reckless. To ensure that he does not stray too far from current thinking, he appends a reference to international law: "Support for freedom fighters is self-defense and totally consistent with the OAS and U.N. charters."

This, it must be admitted, is stretching things. There are two difficulties. How can one plausibly argue that the success of Islamic rebels in Afghanistan is a form of self-defense of the U.S.? The Nicaraguan *contras*, perhaps, might qualify under a generous interpretation of collective security. But Cambodian rebels? Angolans? Eritreans?

Sovereignty

The second problem is that if international law stands for anything, it stands for the idea that sovereignty is sacred. Rebels, by definition, do not have it. The governments they fight, no matter how tyrannous, do. How, ask congressional critics, can one justify violating the sovereignty of other countries by helping overthrow the legitimate government?

The answer must begin with cases. Consider Uganda under Idi Amin. Amin was the legitimate ruler when Tanzania invaded and overthrew him. The Tanzanians might say that this was in response to Ugandan border incursions, but Amin had ordered his troops withdrawn more than a month before Tanzania's action. In any case, if repelling a trespass at the border was the problem, Tanzania should have stopped there. It hardly had to drive to Kampala and install the leader of its choice. Tanzania's action, ridding the world of Amin, was a violation of Ugandan sovereignty. It is hard to see how it can be said to be wrong.

Morally speaking—and congressional critics of the Reagan Doctrine are speaking morally, above all—sovereignty cannot be absolute. Indeed, it is not a moral category at all. Why must it be accorded respect, moral respect, in cases where it protects truly awful regimes? The Nazis were the legitimate government of Germany. That does not mean that one is justified in overthrowing any government one does not like. It does mean that one has to face the crucial question: How awful must a government be before it forfeits the moral protection of sovereignty and before justice permits its violent removal?

In Congress today there is almost no opposition to supporting Afghan and (non-Communist) Cambodian rebels. There is a consensus that resistance to invasion warrants support. But by what logic should support be denied to those fighting indigenous tyranny? It seems curious to decide the morality of a cause on the basis of the address of its chief oppressors.

Relevant Criteria

There are more relevant criteria. First, the nature of the oppression and the purposes of those fighting it. The difference between El Salvador and Nicaragua is that in Salvador, a fledgling democracy is under attack from avowed Marxist-Leninists. In Nicaragua, a fledgling totalitarianism is under attack by a mixture of forces, most of which not only are pledged to democracy and pluralism but fought for just those goals in the original revolution against Somoza.

A second important distinction is whether the insurgency is an authentic popular movement or a proxy force cobbled together by a great power for reasons of realpolitik. In both Salvador and

---

"To be constrained from supporting freedom by an excessive concern for sovereignty (and a unilateral concern, at that) is neither especially moral nor prudent."

Nicaragua, the governments say their opponents are puppets of different imperialisms. In neither case does the charge stick. Consider Nicaragua. As no less a democrat than Arturo Cruz, leader of the (nonviolent) opposition, writes, the *contras*—"the revolt of Nicaraguans against oppression by other Nicaraguans"—now represent an authentic "social movement." Indeed, they are more than 12,000 strong and growing, even after the cutoff of American aid.

If a revolution is both popular and democratic, it is hard to see the moral objection to extending it support. But there is a practical objection: if every country decided for itself which revolutions to support, there would be chaos. What about the prudential reasons for respecting sovereignty and international law?

This argument has the virtue of recognizing that international law is not moral law but an arrangement of convenience: like the social contract in civil society, it is a way to keep the peace. This argument has the vice, however, of ignoring the fact that unlike the domestic social contract, international law lacks an enforcer. It depends on reciprocal observance. If one country breaks the rules at will, then later claims its protection, what—apart from habit and cowardice—can possibly oblige other countries to honor that claim?

Democratic Militance

The idea that international law must be a reciprocal arrangement or none at all is not new. As Churchill said to Parliament in 1940, "Germany is to gain one set of advantages by breaking all the [neutrality] rules [upon the seas]...and then go on and gain another set of advantages through insisting, whenever it suits her, upon the strictest interpretation of the international code she has torn to pieces." He added, "It is not at all odd that His Majesty's government are getting rather tired of it. I am getting rather tired of it myself."

So is today's American Government. There is something faintly comical about Nicaragua going to the World Court to accuse the U.S. of fomenting revolution and interfering in its affairs, when for years the Salvadoran revolution was quite openly headquartered in Managua—and not for a shortage of housing in the Salvadoran jungles. The Reagan Doctrine is more radical than it pretends to be. It pretends that support for democratic rebels is "self-defense" and sanctioned by international law. That case is weak. The real case rests instead on other premises: that to be constrained from supporting freedom by an excessive concern for sovereignty (and a unilateral concern, at that) is neither especially moral nor prudent. The West, of late, has taken to hiding behind parchment barriers as an excuse for inaction when oppressed democrats beg for help. The Reagan Doctrine, while still hiding a bit, announces an end to inaction....

A Nicaraguan friend, an ex-Sandinista who still speaks their language, said in near despair that the struggle of democrats around the world was doomed by the absence in the West of what he called "democratic militance." The Reagan Doctrine represents a first step toward its restoration.

Charles Krauthammer is a senior editor at The New Republic.

The Reagan Doctrine Is Wrong

Eric Patterson and *In These Times*

Editor's note: The following viewpoint is composed of two articles, both of which appeared in In These Times, *an independent socialist newspaper published in Chicago. The first article is written by Eric Patterson, an associate professor of American literature and studies at Hobart and William Smith colleges. The second article is an* In These Times *editorial.*

I

Esteli, the main city in the coffee and cattle country of northern Nicaragua, lies in a high river valley surrounded by rugged hills. The Pan American Highway runs along the outskirts of the city, busy with the commercial traffic that provides the economic basis for the approximately 30,000 people who live there.

Along with the pickups, vans and 18-wheelers there are convoys of military-green jeeps, supply trucks and troop carriers and scores of young men and women in uniform hitching rides. The northern mountains are not only the center of some of Nicaragua's most productive agriculture, but also of the struggles between the revolutionary Nicaraguan government and the counter-revolutionary army sponsored by the U.S. government, the *contras*. . . .

In the U.S. we've heard a lot about Reagan's desire to "put pressure" on Nicaragua, to "turn the screws" on the Sandinistas, but not much about what the actions behind those metaphors really are, what they mean for the proposed appropriations for the *contras*, but we don't know the human cost of the war.

To try to learn this, I interviewed as many people as I could, people from a variety of backgrounds and political orientations: housewives, lay church workers and priests, soldiers, members of rural agricultural coops, nurses, members of the FSLN, owners of small

Eric Patterson, "The Contras: They Can't Win, but They Can Kill," *In These Times*, May 8-14, 1985. Reprinted with permission.

businesses and international volunteers. Time and again I was struck by the friendliness of the Nicaraguans I met and by their willingness to express their views freely. . . .

Peasant Support

Travelling in northern Nicaragua, it becomes clear that the war in that region isn't a civil war. While the *contras* have massive support from the U.S. and well-equipped bases in Honduras and the mountains along the Nicaraguan side of the frontier, they haven't been able to control any population areas—no region or town is defined as *contra*-held territory.

This isn't surprising, given that support for the revolution continues to be strong (as the internationally supervised elections in November, 1984 showed), particularly among the poor peasants, or *campesinos*, who are the chief beneficiaries of the extensive land reform and other social programs. Although the people I met held a wide range of political views—some being quite critical of various Sandinista economic policies—none of them expressed any desire for a *contra* victory. Political slogans of the seven parties that participated in the elections covered the walls in Esteli and the surrounding towns and villages, but none advocated any of the *contra* organizations or leaders.

While the leadership of the *contra* army in the north is largely drawn from that of [Anastasio] Somoza's National Guard, the *contra* troops aren't only ex-guards and mercenaries. Everyone I spoke to said that the *contras* also recruit young Nicaraguans. But it was hard to get a satisfactory explanation of which social groups provide these recruits and why. There is discontent with the revolution, particularly among members of the middle class in Managua and the two old colonial cities, Leon and Granada, who resent the government's adamant protection of the interests of urban and rural workers and the difficulty of obtaining consumer goods due to sharply decreased trade with the U.S.

Toward the end of my stay I had a long talk with a young housing development officer in the Esteli FSLN, named Ronaldo, who offered the most convincing explanations of why people join the *contras*. While some members of the middle class clearly would prefer an economic and political order serving their needs alone and some strongly sympathize with the main *contra* group, the Nicaraguan Democratic Force (FDN), he said he believed very few of them would be willing to make the personal sacrifice of fighting in the mountains.

Christianity and Revolution

Ronaldo's work brings him directly into the conflict—when I spoke with him his right arm was bandaged from a bullet wound he received in a *contra* ambush two days before—and he told me that many of the captured *contras* he sees are young *campesinos*. He explained that most of the *campesinos* are devout Catholics, and that a minority of them dislike the government since they see it as a threat to their faith.

"Although the people I met held a wide range of political views... none of them expressed any desire for a contra *victory."*

Yet he dismissed this fear, and everything I've learned about Nicaragua tends to support him. Although some of the Nicaraguan leaders are Marxists and reject the church, many others are Catholics, including four priests. And while the government has had clashes with the church hierarchy, it continues to have strong support among local priests and nuns, the Christian base communities and much of the laity. The young soldiers and labor volunteers I met all described themselves as Catholics, and the priests and lay church workers all expressed approval of the revolution. Two of the slogans I saw most frequently painted on walls were *"Christianismo y Revolucion son iguales"*—Christianity and Revolution are the same— and *"Entre Cristianismo y Revolucion no hay contradiccion"*—Between Christianity and Revolution there is no contradiction.

Ronaldo explained that despite this alliance, the FDN, much of the Church hierarchy and the right-wing newspaper *La Prensa* have sought to persuade people that the socialist policies of the government do contradict religion, and their *campesino* recruits indicate that they've had some success.

Participants in the Witness for Peace organization, which brings North American clergy to the areas of the worst *contra* violence as a means of deterring further attacks, provided an additional answer to my question. They pointed out that the progress of such major social programs as land reform has been uneven, in part because of the war. Some *campesinos*, particularly those who already own some land and therefore are relatively better off, resent the changes in land distribution that have helped the landless, and so often support and even join the *contras*.

Contra Tactics

Because the *campesinos* aren't solidly behind them in any region and since their overall strategy is to disrupt an economy already weak from years of struggle against the Somoza dictatorship, the *contras* employ hit-and-run tactics against civilians throughout the north. They make sudden attacks on outlying coops, farms and villages, destroying as much equipment and livestock as possible. To drive people out, they instill terror—killing women and children as well as men, and often kidnapping people, torturing them and finally murdering them.

There has been so much violence against civilians since the *contras* began their raids in early 1982 that it's impossible to put together a comprehensive overview of the conflict in the region. But to give some sense of what sort of a war it is, the following is a list of *contra* attacks from June to December, 1984. Throughout those months the *campesinos* who live in the northernmost area, the valley of the Rio Coco, were under almost continuous assault and towns and villages in this region—such as San Juan del Norte, Wiwili, Ocotal, Yali, El Jicaro and Jalapa were struck repeatedly.

In early June...the *contras* attempted to take Ocotal, which is on the Honduran border. They destroyed government offices, a radio station and a major lumber mill, abducted many people and caused the rest of the population fo flee. They were unable to hold the town. Reinforcements of the Nicaraguan army arrived and drove them out after a few hours.

In mid-July there was another major attack, this time much closer to Esteli. The *contras* struck a large agricultural coop, Miraflor, about 10 miles north of the city, and destroyed a $6 million agricultural development project sponsored by the Dutch government. More than 20 *campesinos* were wounded, and the president of the coop and the chief of police of Esteli were killed in the fighting. (Several people to whom I spoke said that the *contras* seek to kill as many leaders as possible in order to create maximum disorder. Whereas the manual the CIA provided for the *contras* euphemistically calls this "neutralization," the *contras* themselves describe it, in an appropriately brutal metaphor, as a policy of *"decapitacion."*)

In early October the *contras* attacked rural coops in the hills east of Esteli—Iziqui, a chicken farm, and La Quinta, a dairy farm, both had to be evacuated and were severely damaged, and another, Las Carbonales, was completely destroyed after its people fled. On

October 21, a quarter of the northern *contra* army (about 3,000 troops) massed against Esteli itself, surrounding the city and bombarding it from the hills to the south. Their mortar fire forced the evacuation of several barrios, and the attack only was driven back when government troops arrived with helicopters.

II

Banana Republics

April 24, [1985] was a sad day for the *contras*," said Secretary of State George Shultz. And it was a day of unaccustomed defeat for the Reagan administration, for that was when the House of Representatives heeded the voice of the American people and turned down Reagan's request for $14 million in additional aid to the CIA-created army in Honduras.

But this administration is determined. It does not take defeat lightly and it fully intends to bring back the days when the Caribbean was an American lake, and when the Central American nations were banana republics that did what they were told to do by their uncle up north. Accordingly, on May 1 President Reagan ordered an embargo on trade with Nicaragua in the hope of "bringing pressure" on the Sandinista government to "mend their ways." The embargo will stop imports from Nicaragua and exports to it, and will end service to the U.S. of Nicaraguan ships and the Nicaraguan airline, Aeronica.

Administration spokesman Larry Speakes explained that this was a necessary act to protect the security of the United States. He gave four specific reasons for the embargo: "Continuing efforts" by Nicaragua "to subvert its neighbors," the Sandinistas' "rapid and destabilizing military build-up," their "close military and security ties to Cuba and the Soviet Union," and their "imposition of Communist totalitarian rule." Consistent with administration policy, three of the four reasons were outright lies and the fourth—about ties to the Soviet Union and Cuba—a half-truth. (A recently published report by the Washington-based Institute for Policy Studies, *In Contempt of Congress*, carefully documents the administration's campaign of lies and misinformation in regard to Nicaragua, as well as El Salvador and Guatemala, by contrasting public statements by administration figures with official documents and reports.)

Yet in striking contrast to the level of opposition to renewed aid to the *contras*, both in Congress and in the media, the administration's new escalation of hostility against Nicaragua seems so far to be meeting little opposition. Unfortunately, this was entirely predictable, for just like the conservatives, most liberals in public life accept the idea that the U.S. has the right to remake the world in its image.

Self-Determination

More aid to the *contras* was voted down because of a widespread apprehension that the administration

was willing, if not eager, to encourage a military escalation that would by design or inexorable logic involve American armed forces directly in a Central American war. This was opposed by some because popular opposition, even at this relatively early stage of hostilities, was too strong, and because the lesson they learned from Vietnam was not to fight a war without solid popular support at home.

Others opposed more aid simply because they though a military solution was wrong. But few members of Congress, and virtually no media pundits seem to believe that former colonial nations like Cuba, Vietnam, and Nicaragua have the right to go their own way unhindered, no matter how unpalatable that way is to those who now hold power in the United States. Even so, that's what self-determination is all about, and that's what this country is supposed to stand for.

As long as another country does not represent an unambiguous threat to our security—and Nicaragua represents no threat at all—our government has no business trying to overthrow its government. The Reagan administration tries to get around the principle by lying about the nature of the threat. Yet there are liberal Democrats, like Rep. Edward P. Boland of Massachusetts, who oppose a military solution, but who still believe that "we should not abandon those who legitimately oppose the Sandinistas," and who want to "keep the *contras* in the game" with non-military aid. In other words, Boland, and those like him in Congress, share Reagan's goal, though they fear his methods. That's why they will not oppose the embargo.

"The contras. . . . instill terror—killing women and children as well as men, and often kidnapping people, torturing them and finally murdering them."

But it is the goal that is wrong, and not only wrong but ultimately unattainable. That is the real lesson of Vietnam. The United States lost that war not because of insufficient military might, but because on the one hand the American people came to understand the nature of the war and to oppose it as a violation of the principles of democracy and self-determination, while on the other the Vietnamese people were fiercely determined to end their colonial status. They could never have won the war if nearly the entire population did not support the Vietcong in this goal.

Collapse of Empires

The same is true in Nicaragua, which is why the *contras* have been unable to hold any territory. They simply do not have enough popular support, even among those disenchanted with the Sandinistas. And, indeed, throughout Central America few people are aware of the history of oppressive domination by the U.S. They would like to get it off their backs.

The world has changed with great speed in this century. We have seen the decline and collapse of all the great 19th-century empires, most notably the British, and the rise of the United States as the last great imperial power. And we have seen the spread of anti-colonial revolution throughout what is now called the Third World. Fifty years ago, before World War II and the Chinese revolution, many people on the left believed that the Soviet Union and the world Communist movement would be the great challenger of Western corporate capitalism and that the world would be bipolar. But as the nature of the Soviet political system became clear, and as the Communist world itself began to diversify, marked most sharply by the Sino-Soviet split in the late '50s, this dream, or nightmare, was put to rest.

"Cold War ideology... threatens all people who believe in democracy because it acts to limit the options to neo-colonialism or to Soviet-style societies."

In fact, today few Third World revolutionary movements look to the Soviet Union as a model for their own revolutions. Certainly the Sandinistas do not. Yet the Reagan administration has revived the bipolar view of the world and is doing its best not only to sell this idea to the American people—the members of Congress seem already sold—but also to impose it on Nicaragua.

Cold War Ideology

That, ultimately, is the function of the embargo. For just as with Cuba after the U.S. cut off shipments of oil in 1960, Nicaragua is now being forced to become more dependent on the Soviet Union for economic support. And no matter what the Sandinista leaders intend, this can only bring them more firmly into the Soviet sphere of influence.

As for the Soviet Union, Reagan's embargo can only give it enhanced prestige among the peoples of the world seeking independence. When their attempts to escape colonial status are being foiled by the United States, the Soviets become the only source of aid to make this possible.

This polarization, and the Cold War ideology that fuels it, threatens all people who believe in democracy because it acts to limit the options to neo-colonialism or to Soviet-style societies. It would be much better for ourselves and for the peoples of the world to let go, to recognize that the dreams of the American Century have turned into a nightmare, and that the days of our empire are as surely numbered as were those of the British empire. Britain survived and lives in peace, and so can we. And if we do let go, the Third World will have a chance really to be a third world and to find its own route to the good society.

Eric Patterson is an associate professor of American literature and studies at Hobart and William Smith colleges and was in Nicaragua three times in 1984. In These Times *is an independent leftist newspaper published in Chicago.*

"The complexities of the situation in Nicaragua, accompanied by a vigorous Sandinista propaganda campaign, have resulted in much confusion about U.S. policy toward Nicaragua."

The US Is the Victim of a Propaganda Campaign

US State Department

In 1979, the Nicaraguan people overthrew the Somoza dictatorship. The Sandinista National Liberation Front (FSLN), which led the military struggle, pledged that it would promote political pluralism, a mixed economy, and a nonaligned foreign policy. Since 1979, the Sandinistas have steered the revolution ever further toward Marxism-Leninism, leaving their original promises unfulfilled. The U.S. Government sought from the outset to build a positive relationship with the new Government of National Reconstruction (GRN), but as the Sandinistas made clear that they had no intention of fulfilling their earlier promises, relations between the two nations deteriorated.

The complexities of the situation in Nicaragua, accompanied by a vigorous Sandinista propaganda campaign, have resulted in much confusion about U.S. policy toward Nicaragua. . . .

U.S. policy is aimed at overthrowing the Sandinista regime.

U.S. policy toward Nicaragua has four objectives:

1) An end to Nicaraguan support for guerrilla groups in neighboring countries;

2) Severance of Nicaraguan military and security ties to Cuba and the Soviet bloc;

3) Reduction of Nicaragua's military strength to levels that would restore military equilibrium to the region; and

4) Fulfillment of the original Sandinista promises to support democratic pluralism and respect human and civil rights.

The Sandinistas are aware of these objectives and know that the concerns of the United States and Nicaragua's neighbors could be met by changes in the behavior of the government in Managua.

The objectives of the United States are consistent

"Misconceptions About U.S. Policy Toward Nicaragua," March 1985. Pamphlet 9417 available from Office of Public Diplomacy for Latin America and the Caribbean, S/LPD, Room 6253, Department of State, Washington, DC 20520.

with the 21 points adopted in September 1983 by the participants in the Contadora process, including Nicaragua.

The Sandinistas are essentially reform-minded nationalists, but U.S. hostility has driven them into the arms of Cuba and the Soviet Union.

The FSLN leadership is composed of committed revolutionaries who openly embrace Marxist-Leninist ideology. They claim to be a vanguard party with a historic right to lead the Nicaraguan people to "socialism" (read: communism). The Sandinistas condemn the United States as the center of capitalism and imperialism and thus the principal obstacle to world revolution. The FSLN hymn proclaims the Sandinista commitment to fight against "the Yankee, enemy of humanity."

Cuban Ties

In a secret speech made in the spring of 1984 to the Nicaraguan Socialist Party (PSN), a Moscow-line Communist party, Sandinista National Directorate member and political coordinator Bayardo Arce acknowledged that the FSLN had never intended to comply with its promises to promote pluralism, a mixed economy, and non-alignment. Arce explained that the FSLN had made these commitments simply to gain international support and thereby forestall possible U.S. intervention. He referred to the elections as "a nuisance" and described the FSLN's goal of building a Socialist Nicaragua with "a dictatorship of the proletariat." Arce closed his speech appealing for "the unity of the Marxist-Leninists of Nicaragua." . . .

The Sandinistas' fraternal relations with the Communist government of Cuba are based both on ideology and the long history of Cuban support for the FSLN. The Sandinistas regard Fidel Castro as their mentor. Not only did he furnish them with a model for their revolution, Castro also provided shelter and training during their 18 years of struggle against Somoza, and he supplied them with the weapons for their final offensive in 1979. Castro has continually coached the Sandinistas, and he even brokered the arrangement among the three FSLN factions which led to the formation of the current National Directorate in March 1979.

Within a week of the Sandinista victory in 1979, Cuba placed about 100 military and security personnel in Nicaragua. Currently, the number of such advisers has swollen to 2,500–3,500. In addition, Cuba has stationed thousands of "civilians" in Nicaragua, including a vast array of technicians and advisers as well as teachers, doctors, and construction workers.

> "The FSLN had never intended to comply with its promises to promote pluralism, a mixed economy, and non-alignment."

In addition to the Cubans, Nicaragua also has at least 200 Soviet and other East-bloc military advisers, and about 50 advisers from Libya and the Palestine Liberation Organization (PLO).

Alternative Alignment

The United States openly distanced itself from the Somoza regime in 1978-79, and in June 1979 cosponsored an Organization of American States (OAS) resolution calling for its replacement. The United States endeavored to foster good relations with the new Sandinista government and offered it an alternative to alignment with Cuba and the Soviet Union. During the GRN's first 18 months, the United States took the leading role in the international effort to assist Nicaragua and authorized $118 million in bilateral aid, far more than any other nation. The United States also supported the flow of $1.6 billion from international financial institutions and Western democracies and the refinancing of Nicaragua's debt to private foreign banks.

Because evidence showed that the Sandinistas were materially supporting the Communist guerrillas in El Salvador, the United States began suspending new aid funds to Nicaragua in late 1980; in April 1981 the United States discontinued economic assistance to the Nicaraguan Government. Despite the strains in our relations, in 1982 the United States offered a new $5.1 million aid package to nongovernmental organizations, but the Sandinistas blocked these programs.

U.S. hostility has compelled the Sandinistas to develop a large military force for its own protection.

The Sandinistas have always intended to establish a

one-party Marxist state with an oversized military. In September 1979, just 2 months after seizing power, the Sandinista leadership met in seclusion for 3 days to map out their plans to consolidate the revolution internally and to promote "revolutionary internationalism." The report of this meeting, "Analysis of the Situation and Tasks of the Sandinista Peoples' Revolution" (commonly referred to as the "72-hour Document"), has been the blueprint which the Sandinistas have followed for more than 5 years.

The Sandinistas, as former guerrilla fighters, planned from the outset to create a large military establishment, closely emulating the Cuban model. Long before any serious armed opposition arose, the Sandinista Peoples' Army (controlled at all levels by the FSLN party) made plans for increasing its manpower, building numerous bases, and training personnel in the use of sophisticated military hardware. The current growth in the Sandinista Army merely continues the decisions made in 1979-1980.

The size of the Sandinista military now exceeds all legitimate defensive needs and is far larger than that of any other Central American country. Their active duty forces are estimated to exceed 60,000, some 5 times the size of Somoza's National Guard at its peak. These troops are supplemented by approximately 60,000 members of reserve and militia units. Moreover, the Sandinistas have acquired huge amounts of Soviet hardware, including at least 340 tanks and armored vehicles, scores of artillery pieces and rocket launchers, patrol boats, and dozens of helicopters, including several MI-24s, the Soviets' top-of-the-line attack gunship.

U.S. actions forced the Sandinistas to implement the State of Emergency which now suspends many of the civil liberties of Nicaraguans.

Long before the Sandinistas faced any threat from armed opposition forces, they were already committing repressive acts....

Sandinista Repression

In February 1981, the Sandinistas arrested numerous Miskito Indian leaders for protesting Sandinista mistreatment of the indigenous population of the Atlantic Coast region. In late 1981–early 1982, the Sandinistas forced approximately 10,000 Miskitos to move from their ancestral homelands to distant resettlement camps. (These and other repressive acts have caused thousands of Miskitos to flee into exile.)

Beginning in 1981, the independent daily *La Prensa* was shut down several times and its owners threatened. The newspaper continues to be censored daily.

In October 1981, five private sector leaders were jailed for 5 months for signing a letter protesting the Sandinistas' actions to implant Marxism-Leninism in Nicaragua.

The Sandinistas imposed the State of Emergency in March 1982, claiming that it was a necessary response to a military threat. In fact, however, the State of Emergency has served primarily to provide the Sandinistas with the legal windowdressing to stifle dissent as they institutionalize their control over Nicaragua. Under its provisions, they have muzzled the free press, restricted the legitimate political activities of opposition parties, and held political prisoners without trial for prolonged periods. The State of Emergency has not been effective in checking the growth of the armed opposition. The many repressive acts committed by the Sandinista Government have actually led thousands of Nicaraguans to join the anti-Sandinista forces.

The April 22, 1984, Pastoral Letter by the Nicaraguan Episcopal Conference refutes the Sandinistas' assertion that U.S. aggression required curtailment of civil liberties. The letter states: "It is dishonest to constantly blame internal aggression and violence on foreign aggression. It is useless to blame the evil past for everything without recognizing the problems of the present."

The United States is seeking a military solution, and charges about the Sandinistas' military buildup and their possible acquisition of MiGs are intended to lay the groundwork for an eventual invasion.

President Reagan has made clear that the United States has no plans or desire to introduce U.S. combat troops into Central America. The United States actively supports the Contadora process aimed at achieving a political solution to the situation in Central America.

Destabilizing the Region

The Sandinistas' military buildup is a major destabilizing element in the region and a matter of grave concern to Nicaragua's neighbors. Costa Rica has no army. Honduras relies on its small air force to offset partially the Sandinistas' overwhelming superiority in ground forces. The introduction of MiGs or other high performance aircraft would neutralize Honduras' only deterrent and further destabilize the region.

At the same time, the United States cannot ignore the fact that the Sandinistas, supported by the Cubans and the Soviets, are carrying out a military-based strategy both internally and externally in the region. It is they who seek a military solution, both for their own internal opposition and for the guerrilla war in El Salvador. . . .

The Sandinistas have attempted to improve relations with the United States while the United States has done nothing in return.

The United States has made numerous attempts to engage the Sandinistas in serious negotiations. Senior U.S. diplomats have traveled to Nicaragua repeatedly to discuss our concerns directly with the Sandinistas.

During his June 1, 1984, visit to Managua, Secretary of State George Shultz designated Special Envoy for Central America, Ambassador Harry Shlaudeman, as the U.S. representative in a projected series of bilateral meetings with Nicaragua. Since that time, Ambassador Schlaudeman has met nine times with Nicaraguan Vice Foreign Minister Victor Hugo Tinoco.

When the Sandinistas have made positive gestures, the United States has responded favorably. For example, in December 1983 Secretary Shultz publicly welcomed the Sandinista announcement of upcoming elections and offer of amnesty for the rebels, expressing hope that these would become a reality. Unfortunately, the Sandinistas' actions, such as continuing to support the Salvadoran insurgents, repression of opposition politicians, harassment of church leaders, and censorship, run counter to their professed willingness to be flexible.

The U.S. is supporting former Somocistas who are spreading terror in Nicaragua.

The vast majority of those now in armed opposition to the Sandinistas had no ties with the Somoza regime, and many were actually Sandinista fighters. The leaders of the armed groups, such as Adolfo Calero and Eden Pastora, were staunch enemies of Somoza and played active roles in the revolution. They and thousands of other Nicaraguans, mostly poor peasants and workers, became disillusioned by the Sandinistas' broken promises and maltreatment of the population. Judging that civic opposition was futile, they have taken up arms to restore the revolution's original goals. They have chosen to risk their lives rather than submit to the Sandinista regime.

"The size of the Sandinista military now exceeds all legitimate defensive needs and is far larger than that of any other Central American country."

The armed opposition has focused its operations on military objectives and some government-owned companies and facilities. Unlike the Marxist guerrillas in El Salvador who have concentrated attacks on economic infrastructure, the Nicaraguan armed opposition has attacked very few economic targets and has sought to avoid civilian casualties. Tragically, the Sandinistas have adopted a practice of mixing civilian government workers with troops in truck convoys, and civilians have been killed when these convoys have been attacked. The Sandinistas are engaged in a propaganda campaign to use such incidents to portray the opposition as human rights violators. It is more likely that the Sandinistas through use of heavy weapons—multiple rocket launchers, artillery, and helicopter gunships— have inflicted far more civilian casualties than have their opponents.

Supporting Violence

Until the Sandinistas began to face armed internal opposition, they had been able to support violence and terrorism elsewhere in Central America with impunity. Only after the Sandinistas themselves began to incur costs from fighting an internal guerrilla movement did they signal a willingness to engage in meaningful negotiations with their Central American neighbors.

Nicaragua's neighbors have never protested that the Sandinistas were assisting insurgents, and the United States has never produced any evidence of Sandinista support for subversion.

The Governments of El Salvador and Honduras have repeatedly denounced the Sandinistas' material support for armed Marxist groups. Guerrilla documents, captured weapons shipments, and statements by guerrilla prisoners and defectors prove continuing Nicaraguan support for Salvadoran insurgents.

"The Nicaraguan armed opposition has attacked very few economic targets and has sought to avoid civilian casualties."

The Honduran military has captured two large groups of insurgents who admitted to having been trained in Cuba and infiltrated into Honduras through Nicaragua. The Sandinistas sent them to initiate armed operations against the democratic government of Honduras.

Costa Rica, a nation without an army, has diplomatically protested numerous incursions by the Sandinista Army into Costa Rica. Protests, both official and private, have been lodged as well over Sandinista support of the radical wing of the legal Costa Rican Communist party, and FSLN support of terrorist actions in Costa Rica.

The United States closely monitors arms trafficking in Central America. While most of this information cannot be released to the public in order to protect intelligence sources and methods, the appropriate committees of the U.S. Congress have reviewed the intelligence and judged that it proves Sandinista material support for guerrillas in the region. . . .

The United States decided well before the Nicaraguan elections took place to brand them a farce. . . .

The Nicaraguan election was seriously flawed, for one party—the FSLN—controlled from the outset every aspect of the process, including the electoral machinery, most of the media, the police, the army, the courts, and mass organizations such as the neighborhood watch committees. The Sandinistas refused to grant the parties of the democratic opposition even the minimal conditions for a genuinely free election and sent mobs to disrupt their meetings. Sandinista supporters staffed the voting stations, registered the voters, and counted the ballots. Two-thirds of the precincts had not a single observer from any party except the FSLN to monitor the conduct of the voting operation and report on irregularities. . . .

The United States has been attacking Nicaragua's human rights record while ignoring serious situations in El Salvador and Guatemala.

The United States has always voiced its concern about the human rights situation in El Salvador and Guatemala, and it sought to use its influence on those governments to curb such abuses. There have been improvements in both countries. In El Salvador, according to information from the Catholic Church, the number of murders committed by right-wing death squads has decreased steadily in the last 4 years with a sharp downturn in 1984. By the end of 1984, they were far lower than the number attributed to the Marxist guerrillas.

Murder and Torture

The human rights situation in Nicaragua is deplorable. The independent Permanent Commission on Human Rights has documented numerous cases of murders, disappearances, tortures, and prolonged detentions without trial for which the Sandinista Government is directly responsible. The Inter-American Human Rights Commission's report for 1983–1984 states that "it is necessary to introduce far-reaching remedies that will bring about unrestricted observance of these rights [to personal freedom, to a fair trial, and to due process], which at this time are significantly weakened."

Following the November elections, the situation deteriorated markedly. The Sandinistas once again imposed heavy censorship of *La Prensa*. The GRN prevented individuals whom it considered its opponents from leaving the country, among them democratic politicians, private sector leaders, union officials, and even a bishop.

The United States has not taken effective steps to encourage democracy and oppose dictators in Central America.

The United States strongly supports democracy in Central America, and this support is yielding positive results.

Honduras in the past 4 years has made the transition from a military regime to a democratic civilian government.

El Salvador has continued the democratic process launched in October 1979, weathering challenges from a violent right and a foreign-supported Marxist insurgency, to hold free elections and install a constitutional civilian government.

Guatemala has committed itself to return to democracy, and in July 1984 elections were held for a constituent assembly. Presidential elections are scheduled for 1985.

Costa Rica continues to enjoy a flourishing democracy.

Of the Central American states, only Nicaragua is moving away from democracy.

In addition to its firm political support for democracy in Central America, in the past 5 years the United States has provided nearly $2 billion of economic aid to stimulate development and about $670 million of military aid to build a shield behind which these fragile democracies can grow.

The underlying reason for the problems in U.S.-Nicaraguan relations is the American concern that a Marxist Nicaragua could become a model for other Central American countries.

The Sandinista seizure of power in 1979 aroused hopes that the Nicaraguan people would soon enjoy a democratic government which would promote social justice and improve the quality of their lives. The Sandinistas, utilizing vast amounts of foreign aid— much of it from the United States—announced a number of programs, including a literacy campaign, construction of clinics, and expanded medical care. The programs were announced with much fanfare, and the Sandinista press releases describing the "miraculous" success of these programs were generally repeated uncritically by the international press.

Had the Sandinistas fulfilled their promises to the Nicaraguan people for better lives and had the new government evolved toward a social democratic system, they possibly might have developed a model that could be emulated. Today none of Nicaragua's neighbors desire to voluntarily copy the Sandinista system. Instead, they fear atttempts by force of arms to impose that system on their countries.

Sandinista Failures

The widely touted literacy and health programs launched by the Sandinistas have not worked as people hoped. To sustain progress in combating adult illiteracy, a continuing effort is required. Initial gains are disappearing for lack of followup and the unavailability of interesting and uncensored reading material. The people are tired of the Marxist propaganda material made available to them in the guise of instructional material. The quality of instruction in the educational system has decreased. In 1983 only a small percentage of graduating secondary school students could pass a standardized examination. This lowering of academic standards is attributable in part to the injection of massive doses of Sandinista political propaganda into the educational program and to the conscription of school age children into the military.

While some advances have been made in preventive health care, the quality of curative medicine in Nicaragua has fallen sharply. The Sandinistas' repressive policies have driven many Nicaraguan doctors, nurses, and medical technicians into exile. Nicaraguans complain that the Cuban personnel who provide much of the medical service in Nicaragua today are poorly trained.

"The human rights situation in Nicaragua is deplorable."

Similarly, the Sandinista claims of expansion of the number of trade unions have not improved the lot of the workers. The creation of new unions under Sandinista control has been a ruse to repress and destroy the free trade unions. The International Labor Organization in March 1984 expressed "serious concern" over the large number of trade unionists and employee representatives arrested and noted that "freedom of association can only be exercised" where fundamental human rights and "freedom from arbitrary arrest are fully respected and guaranteed." Many former trade union leaders have gone into exile.

Despite billions of dollars of foreign aid since 1979, per capita income in Nicaragua has declined to the levels of the early 1960s. Inflation is soaring—an estimated 100 percent in 1984 alone—and workers' wages continually decline in purchasing power.

Whereas Nicaragua, prior to 1979, was a net exporter of foodstuffs, it is now a net importer of food. Production has dropped and Nicaraguans are facing serious shortages of food as well as basic consumer goods. Food is rationed. The issuance of ration coupons by the local Sandinista Defense Committees (CDSs) has become a method of political pressure. Queues, typical of Eastern Europe, are now an everyday sight in Nicaraguan markets. Basic necessities often are available only on the black market at highly inflated prices. Peasant food producers often prefer selling to black market vendors who pay their bills.

In contrast to the poverty affecting Nicaraguan workers and peasants, the Sandinista elite drive luxury cars, and have followed the Soviet example of opening special stores where they can buy goods unavailable to the rest of the population. People elsewhere in Central America are not yearning to have the Nicaraguan model imposed upon them.

The State Department officially supports the anti-Sandinista contras. Its Office of Public Diplomacy for Latin America and the Caribbean publishes pamphlets and speeches about US policy toward Central America.

"Nicaragua is the target of a propaganda campaign whose underlying purpose is to provide a rationale for a deepening U.S. intervention in Central America."

viewpoint 125

Nicaragua Is the Victim of a Propaganda Campaign

Phillip Berryman

In order to win public opinion to its policies, the Reagan administration has sought to give a heroes-and-villains account of what is happening in Central America....

It appears that Nicaragua is the target of a propaganda campaign whose underlying purpose is to provide a rationale for a deepening U.S. intervention in Central America. What follow are responses to the most frequently heard statements of the propaganda campaign.

"The Sandinistas have betrayed the Nicaraguan revolution."

Some Nicaraguans, mainly the upper classes who hoped that after Somoza's downfall they would have the same prestige and power as before, believe that the Sandinistas have betrayed the revolution. Most Nicaraguans, however, view the overthrow of the dictatorship as the first step in a revolution that would reorganize the economy and society so that the needs of the majority would be met. The changes made so far are viewed as a beginning.

"Due to Sandinista mismanagement, Nicaraguans are worse off than they were before."

Some benefits to the people are obvious. During 1980, illiteracy was reduced from 52 percent to 13 percent. School enrollment has doubled. Many formerly landless peasants have received land. Health care has been extended, especially in the rural areas. Mass vaccination campaigns against measles, diphtheria, and polio are fighting those diseases, and malaria has been virtually eliminated.

However, Nicaragua has had to face enormous economic obstacles: a treasury sacked by Somoza and his associates, a foreign debt equaling almost a year's gross domestic product, falling world prices for its exports, and disastrous floods and droughts. In addition, the United States has used its veto power in international lending institutions to block development loans to Nicaragua.

More than 60 percent of the economy remains in private hands, and the government offers credit to businesspeople who seek to keep their enterprises running and to reinvest, and it has sought especially to channel credit to small- and medium-sized businesses and farms....Many large private businesspeople, however, resent what they regard as unjustified government interference....

Despite these obstacles, the United Nations Commission on Latin America states that the Nicaraguan economy grew five percent in 1983 while all other countries in the region showed no growth or a decline.

Meeting Basic Needs

Under difficult conditions the Sandinista revolution has struggled to meet basic needs, while making investments that will provide jobs and greater income. One major accomplishment is that Nicaragua is now self-sufficient in the basic staples of corn and beans. During 1984 it is becoming clear that development is taking second place to survival as Nicaragua prepares to defend itself against what it regards as an almost inevitable attack from the United States.

"The Sandinistas have reneged on their promises to hold free elections."

Most Nicaraguans see their efforts to build a more just society with ongoing grassroots participation (not just at election intervals) as democratic. As a part of this process, they plan to hold elections in November 1984. Some of the previously existing political parties support this process and some do not. Most observers agree that if elections were held today the results would show vast support for the Sandinista revolutionary program.

Phillip Berryman, "Illusions of Villainy," *Sojourners*, August 1984. Reprinted with permission from *Sojourners*, Box 29272, Washington, DC 20017.

"Nicaragua is heading down the familiar road of Marxist totalitarianism."

Nicaraguans insist that their revolution is "Sandinista"—that is, it takes its inspiration from Augusto Cesar Sandino, the nationalist hero who withstood the U.S. Marine occupying force for five years. "Sandinismo" thus emphasizes the nationalistic side of the revolution, its aim to be Nicaraguan and not a copy of any other model.

"If elections were held today the results would show vast support for the Sandinista revolutionary program."

For many Americans "Marxism" is an automatic put-down word; in Latin America, however, Marxist terminology and ideas are as pervasive as psychological jargon is in the United States. Many Latin Americans find that Marxism helps them analyze the roots of their society's problems and the need for structural change. The Sandinistas do not deny the element of Marxism in their policies, but they believe they can use it flexibly and non-dogmatically.

Revolutionary Pluralism

Just as the Sandinistas are seeking to work with a mixed economy, they propose political pluralism. What they have in mind is pluralism within the revolution. The aim is to encourage participation and criticism from those who support the overall direction of the Sandinista revolution.

Nicaragua might seem to be a one-party state, but so is Mexico. From the viewpoint of ordinary citizens, the key question is not so much whether parties compete in particular kinds of elections but whether their governments are responsive and whether they as citizens have a role in shaping policy.

Most Nicaraguans would not judge their government to be totalitarian.

"The press has been suppressed."

In the United States, *La Prensa* has often been portrayed as an independent paper, bravely resisting Sandinista harassment and censorship. This paper did play a major role in the anti-Somoza struggle. However, soon after Somoza's downfall, it began to take an anti-Sandinista line. At that point the bulk of its employees quit *La Prensa* and joined one of its owners in setting up *El Nuevo Diario*.

Many Nicaraguans view *La Prensa* as the voice of the anti-Sandinista elites and even as a tool to undermine the revolution. They see a clear historical precedent in the example of *El Mercurio* in Chile, which received CIA funding and was a major tool for the destabilization campaign that paved the way for

the military overthrow of the elected Allende government.

La Prensa seems to be following a similar model when it gives distorted reporting on food shortages, for example, and so creates a climate of insecurity. The overall line of *La Prensa* is similar to themes of the U.S. government: it creates the impression that Nicaragua is becoming a Soviet-aligned state and that the Sandinistas are hostile to religion; rarely does it find anything to praise in the revolution, and rarely, if ever, does it condemn the CIA-sponsored and -organized attacks on Nicaragua.

In dealing with *La Prensa,* the Sandinista government has tried to maintain a balance between safeguarding free expression on the one hand, and making sure that the revolution is not undermined. Its actions have become increasingly severe:

La Prensa has been closed briefly, and pre-censorship has been imposed to prevent news coverage that might disrupt the country. Many Nicaraguans, very aware of what happened in Chile, agree that these measures are justified; others think that even under adverse conditions, the revolution would be better served by maintaining freedom of expression.

Double Standard

North Americans may be applying a double standard. One researcher found that of eight *New York Times* stories on the Nicaraguan elections scheduled for November 1984, six mentioned the issue of press freedom; and yet, of some 30 stories on the Salvadoran elections filed during the same period, the issue of press freedom was not broached, despite the fact that no opposition press is allowed in El Salvador and journalists have been murdered there. In Guatemala approximately 50 journalists have been murdered, and many others have had to flee, with only minimal interest from the outside world.

"The Sandinista government is repressive and violates human rights."

International human rights commissions of both the Organization of American States and the United Nations have given Nicaragua generally high marks on human rights. Contrary to what has happened after almost all revolutionary victories, no executions of members of the Somoza forces took place. The death penalty was abolished. Those National Guard members convicted of crimes were sentenced to prison; those judged innocent were set free.

Accusations of large-scale atrocities in Nicaragua, when examined, have been found to be without evidence. Human rights organizations such as Americas Watch have expressed concern about arbitrary arrest and detention of people for political reasons. In its report of April 1984, Americas Watch stated that the fate of about 70 Miskito Indians who disappeared in 1982 and some 28 non-Miskitos who disappeared in 1983 had not been clarified. The report points out that these disappearances took place in remote areas and that no case of such disappearances of Miskitos had occurred after 1982. If these people indeed disappeared in the hands of Sandinista forces, it is a severe human rights violation. However, the figure pales by comparison with Guatemala and El Salvador, where tens of thousands have disappeared in recent years. Moreover, in Nicaragua some Sandinista soldiers have been brought to justice for human rights violations.

"The Sandinistas are seeking to destroy genocidally the Miskito culture and people."

Serious problems persist between the Sandinista government and the Miskitos. These are rooted in history, but they have been aggravated by Sandinista errors and exploited by the CIA. Indigenous people—Miskitos, Sumos, and Ramas—and the English-speaking blacks living on the Atlantic coastal plain make up about 4 percent of the Nicaraguan population. Their history has been quite separate from that of the rest of the country. They were colonized by Great Britain. They had little contact with the rest of Nicaragua and were mistrustful of the "Spaniards," as they call those from the Pacific side. The Atlantic side was largely untouched by the anti-Somoza struggle.

Sandinistas' Insensitivity

When the Sandinistas arrived in 1979, they inherited the existing mistrust of the "Spaniards," and their own insensitivity to the particular experience of the people increased that mistrust. In addition, the Miskitos were seeking autonomy in government, land rights, and the rights to natural resources on their lands.

Tensions increased, and events came to a head in February 1981 when the top leaders of the MISURASATA—the name means "Miskitos, Sumos, Ramas, Sandinistas, together—were arrested by the Sandinista authorities. They were soon released, but Steadman Fagoth, the indigenous representative on the Council of State, went to Honduras where he joined ex-Somoza guardsmen in counterrevolutionary activities. Eventually most of the other MISURASATA leaders also left Nicaragua and some became linked to anti-Sandinista groups.

In February 1982, in response to increasing attacks from Honduras, the Sandinistas decided to transfer inland the people living along the Honduran border. As they did so, they destroyed villages to prevent their being used by counterrevolutionary forces. Even those Miskitos who had experienced the cross-border attacks and agreed the transfer was necessary were saddened and angry. An estimated 18,000 Miskitos have left Nicaragua for Honduras out of a total Nicaraguan Miskito population of 80,000. Two thousand have been trained as combatants and are fighting the Sandinistas.

Since the CIA-organized and -financed *contras* would like to seize a portion of Nicaraguan territory, declare it "liberated," and then call for recognition from governments unfriendly to the Sandinista revolution, the "Miskito question" is inevitably part of the larger struggle going on in Nicaragua.

The Sandinistas publicly admit some errors and insensitivity to the indigenous people. Americas Watch, while reporting improvement in relations between the Sandinistas and the Miskitos, states that "serious problems remain."

"The Sandinistas have persecuted the churches and even organized mobs to insult the pope."

The churches find themselves divided over the revolution. Many grassroots pastoral workers see participation in the revolution as a practical consequence of their faith, and many lay church members agree. In addition to the well-known Christian participation of priests in the government, there are many Christian lay people who work with the revolution because they believe it offers the possibility of building a society more in accordance with the gospel. CEPAD, the umbrella organization of Protestant churches, works well with the Sandinista government in development projects.

However, most (but not all) of the Catholic bishops oppose the Sandinista government, fearful that it will become a classic Marxist regime. In their outlook and views, these bishops are quite similar to the anti-Sandinista middle- and upper-class groups. Archbishop Obando y Bravo is the leading public figure opposing the government.

"Many Nicaraguans view La Prensa *as the voice of the anti-Sandinista elites and even as a tool to undermine the revolution."*

This situation offers many opportunities for anti-Sandinista groups, who would simply be rejected if they openly expressed their intention of rolling back the revolution. Religious language and symbols can serve as a code for counterrevolutionary groups.

Religious Symbols

Christians who support the revolution not only regret the use of Christian symbols to serve the counterrevolution, but they also fear that this behavior represents a tragic pastoral failure: the revolution offers the church opportunities for a new kind of evangelization, opportunities that will be missed if the church's leaders use their positions to undermine the revolution.

During March 1983, Pope John Paul II visited Nicaragua in this atmosphere of division. The Sandinista government declared a national holiday and provided bus transportation for all Nicaraguans to Managua (using more than two month's worth of fuel). During his Mass in Managua, the pope said nothing about the accomplishments of the revolution or about the attacks from outside, and showed no sympathy for the sorrow of families mourning the loss of 17 young people killed on the border a few days before. The people became impatient and, as is their custom, began to chant slogans, such as "We Want Peace!" The pope became visibly angry and shouted back "Silence!" three times. All evidence shows that the encounter was spontaneous.

"In addition to the. . . participation of priests in the government, there are many Christian lay people who work with the revolution."

"Nicaraguan 'freedom fighters,' including some former Sandinistas, are seeking to liberate Nicaragua from the Soviet-aligned *comandantes* who have unsurped the revolution."

Since 1979 some former Somoza National Guardsmen have been based in camps in Honduras. In 1983 another group began operating out of Costa Rica. These groups have found some sympathizers and collaborators in the border regions, but their main support comes from the United States.

No revolt exists within Nicaragua. The upper and middle classes are dissatisfied at the loss of their power. On the other hand, some of the poor are dissatisfied at what they see as the slowness of the revolution; for example, the Sandinistas have restrained peasant organizations from simply taking land. But support for the revolution remains strong.

Turn Back Land Reform

The anti-Sandinista groups do not agree on what they propose for Nicaragua. The FDN (Nicaraguan Democratic Front) intends to reverse the Nicaraguan revolution by turning back land reform. Eden Pastora, the military leader of the ARDE (Democratic Revolutionary Alliance), claims his main objection to the Sandinistas is the Cuban influence in Nicaragua. The bulk of the CIA funding has gone to the FDN, but revelations of CIA funding for the ARDE forces as well further discredit Pastora, who is often touted as a hero of the anti-Somoza struggle. His popularity is overestimated in the United States.

By themselves, the anti-Sandinista groups cannot overthrow the Sandinista revolution, and they are incapable of igniting a revolt within Nicaragua, since most people there, whatever complaints they might have about the Sandinistas, recognize that a *contra* government could only be the most extreme sort of repressive dictatorship. *Contra* behavior (killing,

raping, pillaging, destruction) indicates that any government those forces might form would be repressive. Hence, the people do not regard them as "freedom fighters" but as "Somocistas."

Implicitly recognizing that the *contras* were not successful, the CIA in the fall of 1983 moved toward conducting its own operations without Nicaraguan participation (bombing, sabotage, harbor mining).

"With their 2,000 security advisers, the Cubans play a predominant role in Nicaragua."

During most of their struggle, beginning in 1960, the Sandinistas have had only sporadic contact with Cuba. In 1978 when the Sandinistas had become a serious contender for power, the Cuban government showed more interest and provided them with some help. Immediately after their victory, the Sandinistas established close ties with Cuba. Several thousand Cuban doctors and teachers have worked in Nicaragua, and Cuba has helped with development projects such as constructing new sugar mills. However, there are several thousand other foreigners working with the Nicaraguan revolution, including several hundred Americans.

Not Another Cuba

Cubans helped set up the Sandinista security apparatus, undoubtedly drawing on 20 years of experience dealing with U.S. hostility to their country. There is no public evidence for the figure of 2,000 Cuban security advisers. Nevertheless, since much Nicaraguan military equipment is from the Eastern bloc, there may well be a substantial number of Cuban military technicians present.

So far the Nicaraguan revolution differs from the Cuban model in several important respects, reflecting the Sandinistas' recognition that their revolution is unfolding within different circumstances. For example, the stress on a mixed economy in part is a recognition of the shortcomings of the Cuban economy. Despite the fact that several thousand Cuban doctors and health-care workers have served in Nicaragua, the Sandinistas have chosen not to adopt the Cuban doctor- and hospital-centered model of medicine, but to stress village-level health promoters.

One of the most important differences is in the role of religion. In Cuba the churches by and large either served as refuges for those resentful of the revolution or served counterrevolutionary purposes. Consequently, Marxist atheism prevails in public life and practicing Christians cannot be members of the Communist party. In Nicaragua, by contrast, although the Sandinista government is a secular state, religion plays a great role in public life and many Sandinistas are practicing Christians.

"Nicaragua is aligned with the Soviet Union."

The Sandinistas intend to remain non-aligned, partly out of principle and partly out of pragmatism: Nicaragua's most helpful allies have been Western

European democracies, who have provided considerable development aid. When the CIA mining of Nicaraguan harbors was made public, France offered to help clear the mines, and Holland later offered to pay for their clearing. Mexico and Venezuela have offered oil on easy terms, while Argentina and Brazil have offered Nicaragua credit.

Aid from the Soviet Union and some Eastern European countries has been significant. No doubt the Soviet Union would like to see a revolutionary regime in what the United States tends to regard as its "backyard." However, Moscow has made clear it will not put vast sums of money into subsidizing another country like Cuba.

"The Sandinistas are supplying arms to the Salvadoran guerrillas, who maintain their command and control center in Managua."

The Salvadoran insurgency is the outgrowth of a local struggle within El Salvador going back many years, to the early 1970s. Until 1978, El Salvador seemed much more ripe for revolution than Nicaragua.

Since they took power, the Sandinistas have made no secret of their support for the opposition groups in El Salvador. Most Nicaraguans identify with their struggle just as large numbers of other Central Americans draw inspiration from the Nicaraguan revolution. It is also true that Managua serves as a convenient area for Salvadoran, Guatemalan, and Honduran opposition political and diplomatic work (as do Mexico City and San Jose, Costa Rica). No doubt the Sandinista leaders follow the Salvadoran revolution closely and offer advice. We may assume that arms sales may be facilitated in Managua. Nicaragua may function as a kind of "rearguard" (in guerrilla terminology). But this does not make it a "command and control center."

US Intimidation

To date, no convincing public proof exists of continuous and substantial arms shipments from Nicaragua to El Salvador, despite many millions of dollars spent by the United States to monitor and intercept such traffic. Some observers believe significant shipments did take place in 1980.

What seems most plausible is that the Salvadoran insurgents have obtained arms from a variety of sources. Some no doubt passed through Nicaragua, probably with Sandinista involvement. Today the most important source seems to be the Salvadoran official forces themselves, through arms lost in combat or sold by officers. Any Nicaraguan involvement in arms transfers is at the most a marginal element and in no sense should serve to define the problem in Central America.

"With its military buildup, Nicaragua is a security threat to its neighbors."

Nicaraguans regret the effects of their militarization. Ordinary citizens have to do militia drill and leave school or work for months to do patrol, while the development plans of the country are disrupted as resources are diverted into defense.

More than 1,500 Nicaraguans have been killed by counterrevolutionary forces during the last three years. Property has been destroyed, and production has been disrupted. Yet what Nicaraguans fear is that the United States intends ultimately to destroy their revolution by military force. U.S. officials have pointedly refused to rule out attacks on Nicaragua, and the frequent military exercises in the region (such as Ocean Venture II in mid-1984, involving 33,000 U.S. personnel) are clearly designed to intimidate Nicaragua.

Over 100,000 Reservists

Besides its armed forces of about 25,000 troops, Nicaragua has built up a militia of 100,000 or more reservists. (It is curious that no one described the Guatemalan government's creation of a peasant militia involving 400,000 men in 1983 as a threatening "military buildup," despite the Guatemalan army's claim on neighboring Belize.)

"Contra *behavior (killing, raping, pillaging, destruction) indicates that any government those forces might form would be repressive."*

Nicaragua regards its actions as defensive, and military experts who have made on-site examinations concur that its equipment would not serve it for attacks on neighboring countries. For instance, it has virtually no air force. But militarization has its own dynamic. The real threat is that the present postures and actions could escalate into a regional conflagration in which all parties and the people would lose.

"United States efforts toward peace, democracy, and development are thwarted by Nicaragua's refusal to negotiate in good faith."

Both in its rationale and in its actions, the United States administration policy points toward deeper U.S. military intervention. The Nicaraguans see the dispatching of a fleet to Central America with more firepower than all Central American armies combined, and the presence of 5,000 or more U.S. troops in Honduras, as a provocation. This means, in effect, that the U.S. is getting everything ready to use any sort of Nicaraguan action that could be interpreted as "aggression" against Honduras as a pretext for direct attacks on Nicaragua. Articles in the U.S. press have speculated that the United States could defeat the Sandinista army in a matter of days. To the Nicaraguans the U.S. invasion of Grenada looked like a dress rehearsal for an attack on their own country.

These events have impelled other nations, and particularly the "Contadora group"—Mexico, Panama, Colombia, Venezuela—to renew their efforts to find negotiated alternatives. Most governments of Western Europe and Latin America oppose the militaristic thrust of present U.S. policy and urge negotiations.

"U.S. officials have pointedly refused to rule out attacks on Nicaragua, and the frequent military exercises in the region. . .are clearly designed to intimidate Nicaragua."

U.S. government spokespersons have given verbal support to the Contadora initiatives, but U.S. policy has undermined it by announcing or carrying out massive military exercises precisely when Contadora countries were outlining peace proposals. U.S. policy is fundamentally at odds with the Contadora initiatives: if there were mutual agreements banning foreign military advisers, bases, arms shipments, and aid, the United States could be satisfied that there is no Soviet military presence in Central America; the Nicaraguan government could reduce its emphasis on defense and return to development, while the Salvadoran army and government would no longer seem unwilling to accept reciprocity in peace settlements; it is unwilling to acknowledge that its military presence in Central America is foreign.

If there is to be peace in Central America, the United States must recognize that the Nicaraguan revolution is a fact, and that the Sandinista government enjoys broad support among the majority of its people. The Nicaraguans have every reason to want to reach an accommodation with the United States, since their economy, history, and culture are tied to those of the West.

Phillip Berryman is the author of The Religious Roots of Rebellion: Christians in Central American Revolutions *and was the Central American Representative for the American Friends Service Committee from 1976 to 1980.*

bibliography

The following bibliography of books, periodicals, and pamphlets is divided into chapter topics for the reader's convenience. The topics are in the same order as in the body of this *Opposing Viewpoint SOURCE.*

Terrorism

Christopher Andreae — "''I do not accept that there is nothing we can do about terrorism,''' Interview with Paul Wilkinson. *The Christian Science Monitor,* January 31, 1985.

George Ball — "Shultz Is Wrong on Terrorism," *The New York Times,* December 16, 1984.

The Christian Science Monitor — "Terrorism," July 10, 1985.

George J. Church — "An Attack on Terrorism," *Time,* July 1, 1985.

Miles Copeland — "Confrontations of the Third Kind," *National Review,* July 27, 1984.

Don Feder — "Tracking Terrorists Won't Abridge Civil Liberties," *Conservative Digest,* February 1984.

Samuel T. Francis — "Dealing with Terrorists: A Stronger U.S. Policy Is Needed," *Conservative Digest,* November/December 1984.

Robert H. Kupperman and David Williamson Jr. — "Fighting Terrorism with Violence Isn't a Solution—It's an Invitation," *The Washington Post National Weekly Edition,* December 17, 1984.

Hans Lebrecht — "Fighting Terrorism," *Daily World,* June 25, 1985.

Cord Meyer — "What Must We Do Next: Anti-Terror Moves Required at Home," *The Washington Times,* July 3, 1985.

Joe Pichirallo and Edward Cody — "America's Secret War on Terrorism in Other Countries," *The Washington Post National Weekly Edition,* April 8, 1985.

Saundra Saperstein — "Washington's Security Blanket," *The Washington Post National Weekly Edition,* January 7, 1985.

George Shultz — "U.S. Government and Business: Our Common Defense Against Terrorism," February 4, 1985. Available from the United States Department of State, Bureau of Public Affairs, Washington, DC 20520.

George Shultz — "Terrorism and the Modern World," *Department of State Bulletin,* December 1984.

Mark Whitaker and others — "Ten Ways to Fight Terrorism," *Newsweek,* July 1, 1985.

Kenneth Woodward and others — "Islam Versus the West," *Newsweek,* June 24, 1985.

C. Robert Zelnick — "Combating International Terrorism," *The Christian Science Monitor,* July 10, 1985.

US/Africa

America — "Meanwhile, the Children Starve," December 15, 1984.

Thomas Bartholomay — "Control Data and Apartheid," *Science for the People,* March/April 1984.

Carole Bass — "The Unions and South Africa," *The Progressive,* June 1985.

Richard K. Bennett — "Why Ethiopia Is Starving," *Reader's Digest,* May 1985.

Donald M. Blinken — "To Divest in South Africa, or Not?" *The New York Times,* June 6, 1985.

Christianity and Crisis — "South Africa: No Business Is Good Business," September 17, 1984.

Goodwin Cooke — "What Food Aid Does Not Do for Africa," *Los Angeles Times,* February 19, 1985.

Christianity Today — "Africa's Need for Food Tests Limits of US Emergency Aid," February 1, 1985.

Alan Cowell — "Defiance in South Africa," *The New York Times Magazine,* April 14, 1985.

Chester A. Crocker — "The U.S. Response to Apartheid in South Africa," April 17, 1985. Available from the United States Department of State, Bureau of Public Affairs, Washington, DC 20520.

Kenneth W. Dam — "South Africa: The Case Against Sanctions," April 16, 1985. Available from the Department of State, Bureau of Public Affairs, Washington, DC 20520.

Jennifer Davis — "The Cyclone Is Coming," *The Progressive,* February 1985.

Nick Eberstadt — "Famine, Development & Foreign Aid," *Commentary,* March 1985.

David L. Goodman — "South Africa Digs In for a Long Stay," *The Nation,* May 11, 1985.

The Heritage Foundation — "An Investment Strategy to Undermine Apartheid in South Africa," *Backgrounder,* April 30, 1985. Available from the Heritage Foundation, 214 Massachusetts Ave. NE, Washington, DC 20002.

The Heritage Foundation — "A Plan for Rescuing Starving Ethiopians," *Backgrounder,* December 27, 1984. Available from the Heritage Foundation, 214 Massachusetts Ave. NE, Washington, DC 20002.

Vicki Kemper — "The Movement to End U.S. Support of South African Injustice," *Sojourners,* February 1985.

Elwood E. Kieser	"A Visit to Ethiopia," *America*, January 16, 1985.
Richard D. Lamm	"Attach Strings to Emergency Relief," *The New York Times*, April 17, 1985.
Harold Marcus	"The Politics of Famine," *Worldview*, March 1985.
Jean Mayer	"Preventing Famine," *Science*, February 15, 1985.
William C. Norris	"South Africa: Let's Not Divest Blindly," *Los Angeles Times*, June 6, 1985.
Alan Paton	"South Africa Is in a Mess," *The New York Times*, April 3, 1985.
Lynn Scarlett	"Death in Ethiopia: Who's to Blame?" *Reason*, May 1985.
J.D. Sethi	"The Politics of Hunger," *World Press Review*, February 1985.
William Steif	"Tales of Apartheid," *The Progressive*, February 1985.
Matthew Stevenson	"Old South Africa," *American Spectator*, June 1985.
Stephanie Urdang	"Removals: Destroying Communities to Cheapen Labor," *Christianity and Crisis*, February 4, 1985.
Sylvia Vollenhoven	"Apartheid's Uncle Toms," *Mother Jones*, July 1985.

US/Central America

Diego Arria	"Why They Paint 'Yanqui Go Home,'" *The New York Times*, June 30, 1985.
Humberto Belli, Adolofo Calero, and Haroldo Montealegre	*Three Nicaraguans on the Betrayal of Their Revolution*, 1985. Pamphlet available for $4 from Heritage Foundation, 214 Massachusetts Ave. NE, Washington, DC 20002.
Phillip Berryman	*The Religious Roots of Rebellion*. Maryknoll, New York: Orbis Books, 1984.
Raymond Bonner	"The Case for Letting the Sandinistas Alone," *Los Angeles Times*, April 14, 1985.
Joel Brinkley and Bill Keller	"US Military Is Termed Prepared for Any Move Against Nicaragua," *The New York Times*, June 4, 1985.
Abraham Brumberg	"'Sham' and 'Farce' in Nicaragua? Documentary Evidence on the Nicaraguan Election," *Dissent*, Spring 1985. Available from Foundation for the Study of Independent Social Ideas Inc., 521 Fifth Ave., New York, NY 10017.
George Bush	"Nicaragua: A Threat to Democracy," *Department of State Bulletin*, May 1985.
Central Intelligence Agency	*Freedom Fighter's Manual*. Available for $2 from Grove Press, Inc., 196 W. Houston St., New York, NY 10014.
Congressional Digest	"US Policy Toward Nicaragua: Pro & Con," November 1984.
Mark Falcoff and Robert Royal	*Crisis and Opportunity: US Policy in Central America and the Caribbean*. Washington, DC: Ethics and Public Policy Center, 1984.
Timothy Garton Ash	"Back Yards," *New York Review of Books*, November 22, 1984.
David Gergen	"Storm Over Nicaragua," *U.S. News and World Report*, March 11, 1985.
Robert S. Leiken	"Nicaragua's Untold Stories," *The New Republic*, October 8, 1984.
Michael Massing	"Hard Questions on Nicaragua," *The Nation*, April 6, 1985. See also April 20 issue for responses to Massing's article.

Joel Millman	"Reagan's Reporters: How the Press Distorts the News from Central America," *The Progressive*, October 1984.
Newsweek	"Playing for Time," May 13, 1985.
The New York Times	"America's Choices in Nicaragua," April 21, 1985.
Bernard Nietschmann	"The Unreported War Against the Sandinistas," *Policy Review*, Summer 1984.
Daniel Ortega	"Why the US Must End Its War," *The New York Times*, March 13, 1985.
George Shultz	*America and the Struggle for Freedom*. Pamphlet available from Bureau of Public Affairs, US Department of State, Washington, DC 20520.
U.S. News and World Report	"Pro and Con: Should US Help Oust Nicaragua's Government?" April 1, 1985.

index

abortion bombings
  as terrorism, 17
Abramoff, Jack, 77
Afghanistan, 53
  US involvement in, 3
Africa
  apartheid, 45-68
    and disinvestment
      benefits of, 55-57, 67-68
      harmfulness of, 59-61, 63-65
    compared to Nazi Germany, 47, 67
      as fallacy, 49, 53
    inhumanity of, 45-48
    improvements in, 49-53
    ways to improve
      constructive engagement, 49
        failure of, 37, 68
      Sullivan Code, 51, 56, 63-64
        failure of, 67
  famine, 33-43
    and food aid
      harmfulness of, 36
      need for
        better organization, 35, 42
        immediate, 33
    causes of
      communist government, 37-40
      overpopulation, 41-43
    ways to solve
      massive food aid, 33
      pressure on communist
        government, 42
Americas Watch, 94, 95
Arafat, Yasser, 29
ARDE (Democratic Revolutionary Action),
  71-72, 96
Arnold, Terrell, 17
atomic bombings, 2

Berryman, Phillip, 93
Bishop, Maurice, 7
Boland, Edward P., 85
Boston Tea Party, 19
Botha, P.W., 50, 55, 57, 59
Brown, Lester, 41
Bundy, McGeorge, 69
Buthelezi, Gatsha, 53, 56

Calero, Adolfo, 89
capitalism
  and terrorism, 1-3
  as force behind apartheid, 64
  need to abolish, 12
Carter, Jimmy, 21, 51, 80
Castro, Fidel, 87-88
Choyke, William J., 63

Churchill, Winston, 81
CIA (Central Intelligence Agency), 76
  and Miskito Indians, 95
  failure to counteract terrorism, 9
  growing influence of, 11
  involvement in
    Chile, 2
    Indonesia, 2
    Iran, 22
    Lebanon, 25-26
    Nicaragua, 2, 69, 77, 96
Clark, William, 36
Clausewitz, Karl Von, 6
Coffin, William Sloane, 53
Cold War ideology, 86
communism
  as cause of African famine, 37-40
  in Nicaragua, 70
  US policy toward, 75-77
    failure of, 86
constructive engagement, 49
  failure of, 57, 68
Contadora group, 70
  attempts at negotiations, 98
  US support of, 87
    myth of, 98
contras
  and the Congress, 77, 85
  as ex-Somocistas, 83, 96
    myth of, 89
  attacks on civilians, 84, 96, 97
    myth of, 89
  popular support of, 72
    myth of, 85-86
  tactics of, 84
  US support of, 75-77
    as positive, 71-73
    as negative, 69-70
    need for, 71-73
corporations, US
  as a force for change, 63-65
    myth of, 67-68
  should leave South Africa, 67-68
covert action
  failure of, 70
  immorality of, 69
  need for, 79
Crusaders, 1
Cuba
  aid to Nicaragua, 87, 89, 91
    exaggeration of, 96
  as Nicaraguan model, 87-88
  involvement in terrorism, 13, 17
  missile crisis, 70
  US involvement in, 86
Cuellar, Javier Perez de, 2, 34

D'Amato, Al, 38-39
D'Aubisson, Roberto, 3
democracy, 6, 14
Department of Defense, 14
disinvestment, see South Africa
Dresden, 2

El Salvador
  human rights in, 90
  Nicaraguan support of, 7, 97
  US involvement in, 2, 3
Ethiopia
  famine, 33-36
    aid
      as undermining self-sufficiency, 36
      delay in, 33, 35
      internal government misusing, 38,
        39, 42
      political overtones, 35
    causes of
      communism, 37-40
      internal government, 34, 35-38
      population, 41-43
        insignificant, 42
    ways to relieve
      massive agricultural development,
        36, 41, 42
  relocation program of, 39
Ethiopian Relief and Rehabilitation
  Commission, 38

Fadlalla, Mohammed Hussein, 23
Falcoff, Mark, 71
famine, see Ethiopia
FARN (Nicaraguan Armed Revolutionary
  Forces), 71-72
FDN (Nicaraguan Democratic Force),
  71-72, 84, 96
Felt, Mark, 9
foreign policy
  as weapon against apartheid, 68
Francis, Samuel T., 8
Freud, Sigmund, 6
FSLN (National Liberation Front), 84, 87,
  90

Garvin, Glenn, 17
Grenada
  US involvement in, 2
    as liberation, 7, 8
Griffin, Keith, 37
Gromyko, Andrei, 2
Guatemala
  human rights in, 90
Gvozdev, Yuri, 1

Hall, Tony, 33
Hart, Jeffrey, 37
Hasan, Sabah, 19
Helms, Richard, 9
Heritage Foundation, 37
Hinckley, John, 5
Hiroshima, 2
Honduras
  contras in, 83
  US military aid to, 97
human rights
  and US intervention, 11-12

In These Times, 83
Indonesia, 2
Institute for Policy Studies, 85
Inter-American Human Rights
  Commission, 90
IRA
  as evil, 30, 31
Iran
  as terrorist state, 21-22, 23, 30
  attempts to end terrorism, 24
  hatred of the US, 21-22
  need for US to ease tensions with, 23-24
Israel
  invasion of Lebanon, 26-27
    as good, 31
Italy, 14

Jackson, Michael, 64
Jacobson, Philip, 37
Japan, 2
Jenkins, E.R., 50
Johnson, Paul, 29, 49

Kgama, S.I.P., 61
Khomeini, Imam, 22
Kirkpatrick, Jeane J., 5, 77
Kissinger, Henry, 52
Koch, Noel C., 13
Krauthammer, Charles, 79
Kupperman, Robert, 18
Kuwait, 14

La Prensa
  suppression of, 84, 88, 90
    exaggeration of, 94
Leach, Jim, 76
Leahy, Patrick, 35
Lebanon
  bombing of, 2, 26-27
    as good, 2
  US should pull out, 27
Lee, Robert W., 37
Libya
  as terrorist state, 30
Lincoln Review, The, 59
Lisker, Joel, 20
Luthuli, Albert, 56

Mandela, Nelson, 56
Mariam, Mengistu Haile, 35, 37, 38
Marines
  terrorist attack on, 13, 21
Marxism, 94
Maynes, Charles William, 25
McFarlane, Robert C., 77

McManus, Doyle, 75
media
  and terrorism, 1, 19
  as misinformed, 38
Mehlomakulu, Llewellyn, 60
Michaels, David A., 1
Middle East
  need for US to pull out, 27
  need for US to seek reconciliation, 21-24
  terrorism in, 13, 19-20
  US failure in, 9
Miskito Indians
  and CIA, 95
  Sandinistan treatment of, 72, 88
    exaggeration of, 94-95
MISURASATA, 95
Mugabe, Robert, 52

National Guard, 71
National Security Decision Directive 138,
  11
Nicaragua
  afraid of US overthrow, 97
  and Cuba, 87-88, 89, 91
  as budding democracy, 93-94
  as exporter of revolution, 83, 90
    myth of, 97
  CIA in, 2, 69, 77, 96
  contra attacks in, 84-85, 89
  Sandinistan government
    antagonism toward US, 89
    as terroristic, 1
    improvements of, 83, 90, 93
    military build-up
      as defensive, 97
    popular support of, 96
    support of El Salvador, 7, 97
  Soviet involvement in, 70, 73, 87, 89
  US involvement
    as bad, 69-70
    as immoral, 48
    necessity of, 71-73
    trade sanctions, 85, 86
Nixon, Richard, 73
  doctrine of, 80
North, James, 55
Nygard, Richard, 40

O'Neill, Thomas P., 71
Oppenheimer, Harry, 51
Orwell, George, 6, 8

Palestinian Liberation Organization, 29, 31
  support of Nicaragua, 88
Pastora, Eden, 71, 89
  murder of, 5
Paton, Alan, 52
Patterson, Eric, 83
Pinochet, Augusto, 2
Poland, 48
Pope John Paul II
  assassination attempt, 15
  visit to Nicaragua, 95-96
PSN (Nicaraguan Socialist Party), 87

Reagan, Ronald, 2, 69-70
  and Nicaragua, 72, 85, 89
  anti-terrorist policies, 9, 75-77, 86, 93

  as immoral, 22, 49, 56, 83-86
  effectiveness of, 78-81
  ineffectiveness of, 11-12
  doctrine of, 75-77
  soundness of, 79-81
  wrong, 83-86
revolutions
  in Central America, 80, 84
Robinson, Jackie, 45

Sakharov, Andrei, 53
Sandinistas
  as communists, 87
    myth of, 94, 96
  attacks on civilians, 90
  Catholic opposition to, 95
  human rights violations committed by,
    88-89, 90
  myth of, 93, 94
  exporters of revolution, 90
  improvements made by, 93
  military force of, 88
  misuse of aid, 91
Sandino, August Cesar, 94
Shultz, George P., 9, 11, 25, 77, 79, 85, 89
  and Nicaragua, 12
slavery
  as terrorism, 1, 30
Solarz, Stephen J., 76, 77
soldiers, 5
Solzhenitsyn, Alexander, 8
Somoza, Anastasio Debayle, 71, 83, 87
South Africa
  apartheid, 45-68
  and disinvestment
    benefits of, 55-57, 67-68
    harmfulness of, 59-61, 63-65
  compared to Nazi Germany, 47, 67
    as fallacy, 49, 53
  inhumanity of, 45-48, 53
  improvements in, 49-53, 59
  ways to improve
    constructive engagement, 49
      failure of, 37, 68
    Sullivan Code, 51, 56, 63-64
      failure of, 67
  democracy unsuitable, 51
  disinvestment
    reasons against, 51, 53
      cannot improve apartheid, 67-68
      harms blacks, 59-61
    reasons for
      aiding blacks, 55-57
      can improve apartheid, 63-65
    supported by Africans, 56
      myth of, 52, 60
  drought in, 52
  government
    destroying black history, 45-46
    oppression through language, 46
    shooting blacks, 46-47
  homelands in, 51
  human rights eroded, 68
    myth of, 59
  oppression of blacks, 45
  settlement of, 45-46
  uprisings in, 55, 64
  US should leave, 67

Soviet Union
    aid to Ethiopia, 35, 39
    as model for revolution
        myth of, 80
    as terrorists, 6, 9, 13, 15
        as lie, 2, 3
    involvement in Eastern Europe, 8, 15
    support to Nicaragua, 96
    support to the PLO, 29
    US opposition to, 76
Speakes, Larry, 85
Stalin, Josef, 7
Sullivan Codes, 51, 56
    effectiveness of, 63-64
        unsuccessful, 67
Sullivan, Leon H., 63
Symms, Steven D., 77

Taylor, Humphrey, 59
terrorism
    and capitalism, 1-3
    and the PLO, 29-31
    and totalitarianism, 5-8
    as attack on US, 18
    as crime, 7, 10
    chemical, 18-19
    control possible, 13-15
        as impossible, 17-20
    getting worse, 13
    government's right to squelch, 8
    in Iran, 21-24, 29, 30
    in Lebanon, 25-27
    innocent victims of, 5, 6, 13, 16-18
    in the US, 1, 17, 18, 19
    politics of, 5, 6
    successes of, 15
    US need to fight, 9-10, 30
        as threat to human rights, 11-12, 23
            impossibility of, 11-12
    US-sponsored, 25-27
terrorist states
    emergence of, 30
    need for US to pull out, 25-27
    need for US to seek reconciliation with,
        21-24
    need for US to punish, 29-32
Thomas, Franklin, 67
Tinoco, Victor Hugo, 89
Truman, Harry S, 73
    doctrine of, 79
Turkey, 14
Tutu, Desmond, 45, 52, 56
    support of disinvestment, 68

Ulc, Otto, 49
United Nations
    as useless, 31
    condemnation of US, 8
    inadequacy of, 39
    Soviet proposal before
        as good, 2-3
        as propaganda, 8
US
    and Ethiopian famine, 37-38, 39
        aid to alleviate, 42
            should be stopped, 40
            slow to respond, 35
    and Nicaragua, 69-98

    and Contadora process, 98
    attempts to overthrow government, 97
        myth of, 87, 93-98
    need to combat communism, 79-81, 86
    should recognize Sandinistan
        government, 98
    supporting democracy, 90-91
    support of the contras, 75-77
        immorality of, 69-70, 83-86
        morality of, 71-73, 85, 87
    trade sanctions, 86
and South Africa
    corporations
        as a force for change, 63-65
            myth of, 67-68
    disinvestment
        reasons against, 51-52, 59-61
        reasons for, 55-57
and terrorism, 9-10, 21
    attacks against, 18
    ineffective policies of, 9, 13-15
    ways to deal with terrorist states
        covert action, 9-10
            immorality of, 11-12
        pulling out, 25-27
        punishment, 29-32
            as violation of human rights,
                11-12, 23
        reconciliation, 21-24
            failure of, 25
        responsibility for, 17, 21-22
hostage crisis, 21, 26
terrorism in, 1, 17, 18, 19

Vietnam
    lessons of, 85
    state-sponsored terrorism in, 7
    US involvement in, 1, 3, 76, 79
        as bad, 12

War Powers Act, 72
Watson, Russ, 33
Webster, William, 3
Weicker, Lowell, 56
Weinberger, Caspar W., 77
Wharton, Clifton R. Jr., 49, 52, 67
Witness for Peace, 8
Wright, Robin, 21

Zonis, Marvin, 21